Gardening Wizardry for Kids

L. Patricia Kite
Illustrated by
Yvette Santiago Banek

BARRON'S

Dedication
With love to Laura Elena Kite-Raney,
who has always been such a blessing.

All inquiries should be addressed to:
Barron's Educational Series, Inc.
250 Wireless Boulevard
Hauppauge, New York 11788

Library of Congress Catalog Card No.: 94-37729

International Standard Book No. 0-8120-1317-4

Library of Congress Cataloging-in-Publication Data

Kite, L. Patricia.
    Gardening wizardry for kids / by L. Patricia Kite.
        p.   cm.
    Includes bibliographical references (p.   ) and index.
    ISBN 0-8120-1317-4
    1. Fruit-culture—Juvenile literature. 2. Vegetable gardening—Juvenile
    literature. 3. Herb gardening—Juvenile literature. 4. Indoor gardening—
    Juvenile literature. 5. Fruit—Juvenile literature. 6. Vegetables—
    Juvenile literature. 7. Herbs—Juvenile literature.
    8. Garden fauna—Juvenile literature. 9. Nature craft—
    Juvenile Literature. [1. Gardening] I. Title
    SB357.27.K58   1995
    635'.048—dc20

                                    94-37729
                                    CIP
                                    AC

PRINTED IN HONG KONG
5678   9927   98765432

Contents

Preface

Gardening Wizardry for Kids was written for the many children today whose garden growing space may be only a windowsill, whether it be in an apartment, a classroom, or a home surrounded by concrete. The projects and experiments in this book can be accomplished by children of all cultures without a lot of monetary expenditure, space requirements, or working-parent time—but with great success.

But *Gardening Wizardry for Kids* offers more than a compilation of easy-to-read, easy-to-do plant projects and experiments for home and school. For the child comparing apple seed numbers, there is also the history of apples, apple folklore, and apple games. For the bean seed grower, there are Native American legends, bean crafts, and ample growth experiments. A favored fruit or vegetable is almost certain to have a story presented and a fact-finding indoor gardening use.

Herbs, so much a part of early medicines, have their own chapter: history, growing instructions, and even ideas of how to use the aromatic results in daily meals. The child working on a project of this kind can quickly access information from this one book.

There are "extras," too. Like homegrown earthworms, a gift orange pomander, and a list of places in the United States or Canada that will send seed catalogs.

Gardening Wizardry for Kids is a practical "do-it" book, but it is also an excellent reference book for the learning child or for the adult who loves plants.

Note to Parents and Teachers

The herbal remedies mentioned in this book were used before modern medicine. Many of these remedies have been found to be useless and some may even be quite harmful. Even ordinary herbs can cause an allergic reaction in some people. Our ancestors had no choice in medicines, so they tried almost anything.

Herbal remedies are mentioned in this book for their historical context only. Nothing in the text is intended to be diagnostic or prescriptive. For medical problems of any kind, consult a physician. The author and publisher assume no responsibility for reader use of any herb or spice. (All projects and experiments are to be done with adult guidance and aid, as necessary.)

History and Folklore of Common Fruits and Vegetables

1

General History of Food Plants

The first people searched for and ate parts of wild plants. In ancient campsites and caves, archaeologists find that early meals included grass seeds as well as seeds of what might be considered weeds today: ribwort, hemp nettle, and corn spurrey.

As time passed, early people realized that if seeds were collected and planted in certain places, they wouldn't have to be searched for. Searching took a lot of time. Searchers also faced dangers from wild animals.

With the beginning of ancient farms, people were able to stay in one place, instead of having to move when the area food supply was used up. According to noted Swiss botanist Augustin de Candolle (1778–1841), apples, apricots, beans, cabbage, and onions are among the 50 plants that have been cultivated in some form for over 4,000 years.

Over many centuries, people of long ago discovered that some plants of each kind grew better than others. The farmer began to save the seed of the best.

Food crops usually spread from one area to another by way of land travel. But a huge ocean separated the Old and New Worlds. Columbus is not often thought of as a food distributor. But on his first ocean voyage, he carried native corn from the New World back to Europe by way of Spain. On his return to the Americas, his ships carried seeds of European crops. His name appears in many garden history books that recorded fruits and vegetables growing where his ships landed.

Plants originating in the United States include strawberries, blackberries, raspberries, plums, the American grape, and the pumpkin.

Apples date back to prehistoric times. The earliest known types were walnut-size crab apples growing in forested areas of Asia and Europe. By the time people began keeping crop records, apples looked something like we know them today. They are thought to be our oldest cultivated, or cared for, fruit.

Apple trees were prized in ancient Greek and Roman gardens. The Roman emperor Julius Caesar particularly liked plants. After the Romans conquered Britain, about 2,000 years ago, his soldiers planted many apple trees. Residents called them the stamp of Rome, and the trees became a symbol of Roman occupation.

After the Romans left Britain, other tribes came in. The Roman gardens were left behind. But apple trees are hardy. Even without a lot of care, they continued to grow.

In the 1600s, British students studying for religious careers also had to study plants. One such student was William Blackstone. After graduation, he began trying to create different kinds of apple trees.

Apple

Pyrus malus

In the meantime, various religious groups had begun creating colonies in North America. William Blackstone was chosen to head one of these groups. He arrived in Boston Harbor in 1623, with Bibles and a bag of apple seeds.

The members of his flock hated the cold, the wilderness, and the mosquitoes. The next year they left. Blackstone stayed on by himself, with his baby apple trees.

A different religious group arrived. Blackstone was unhappy with the changes and chose to leave. Taking his apple seeds, he went to Rhode Island. Baby trees quickly appeared there after his arrival. Apples soon grew throughout New England. By 1650, any important gentleman of the Puritan faith was dealing in apple trees.

As America grew, so did apple trees. Every farm had several. Fallen apples went to feed cattle and horses. Apple bark could be simmered in water to make yellow dye for clothing. There were apples for cooking, apples for eating, apples for cider.

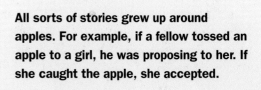

All sorts of stories grew up around apples. For example, if a fellow tossed an apple to a girl, he was proposing to her. If she caught the apple, she accepted.

Early Americans used a lot of cider. Although American stream and river water was good, this wasn't true in Europe, in their home countries. Back in Europe, the water was full of germs. People didn't understand about germs back then. When someone died of the plague, for example, family members threw sheets and blankets into the river. Anybody who drank water from an open source usually got sick. People blamed this on fresh water itself. So the pioneers drank cider, or liquid pressed from apples, instead.

A farm woman invented apple pie. She flavored it with fresh maple syrup and spices.

Every covered wagon moving west carried apple seeds. Some apples have very good storing power. They were often the only fresh fruit available in winter. The apples were buried before the ground froze, then dug out as needed until spring. Women and children also peeled, then sliced, apples. These apples were dried in the summer sun, put in cotton bags, and hung from chimney corners or attics until needed.

Have you ever heard the saying "An apple a day keeps the doctor away"? The apple is Michigan's state tree. So 1,300 Michigan students once tested this health idea by eating an apple a day for three years. They did have fewer colds. Apples contain vitamin C, vitamin A, and potassium, so maybe they helped.

America is now the second biggest apple growing country in the world. Only France comes first. How many types of apples do you find at the market? You might find about five types, depending on where you live. But there are over 10,000 apple types in the world, many grown in home gardens. They just don't ship well. But you may find them at farmers' markets. Take a look.

Pioneer Apple Games

Pioneer children played apple games, such as "fortune telling," with apple seeds. Every child in the game placed a single apple seed on each cheek. One seed was called home, *the other* travel. *If the travel seed fell off first, the child would never travel anyplace. If the home seed fell off first, the child would get to go wandering around the world.*

In another game, each child playing collected and named five apple seeds. The child then placed these named seeds on her or his face. The first apple seed to fall showed which person the child would marry.

Another marriage future game was played by each child taking five apple seeds. Boys gave their seeds girls' names. Girls gave their apple seeds boys' names. The lightweight seeds were then thrown toward the ceiling. If a seed hit the ceiling, you would marry the person named.

Guessing a mate was very popular with the apple-loving early settlers. Even apple peels got into the picture. An apple was peeled with a knife without breaking the peel. To break the peel was bad luck. The person would then twirl the peel around the head three times. Then the peel would be lightly tossed from the twirling finger over a shoulder and onto the floor. When it landed on the ground, it would seem to form an initial. That would be the initial of your future husband or wife.

When toys were few and apples were plentiful, children became quite imaginative as to their use. "Snap apple" was a game that didn't predict a mate. A string was tied onto an apple stem, then attached to a doorway. The children would line up and try to bite into the swinging apple. Have you ever tried this? It's harder than it looks.

Johnny Appleseed

Do you remember hearing about Johnny Appleseed? He was a real person, and his real name was John Chapman. He was born in Leominster, Massachusetts, on September 26, 1774.

When he was twenty-three years old, John started his travels westward. First he began planting quick-growing apple trees on land he someday hoped to farm. It was one way of staking a claim.

But as he walked through the wilderness, John realized that although the pioneers moving westward had room for apple seeds in their covered wagons filled with furniture and supplies, there was no room for apple trees. John was a quick-thinking businessperson. Alone, he could move more quickly, either by canoe or on foot. He decided to get a year or so ahead of the covered wagons.

Here and there, where the land seemed right, in Ohio, Pennsylvania, and Indiana, John planted apple seeds collected from cider mills. He planted hundreds of thousands of these seeds. When the covered wagons arrived, he sold the growing trees to the settlers for about 6½ cents each. That let them have food and cider apples more quickly.

During the War of 1812, John became a scout in Ohio, warning farm families of raids so they could escape. A peaceful man, he disliked all warfare and became very religious. He did a lot of preaching along the way. But he also had a lot of skill with both animals and plants. If he came across a home where someone was sick, he often treated that person with herb medicine.

As John grew older, payment for his trees meant less and less. He took whatever was offered, often food or something to wear. He planted apple seeds along trails and streams. Some were great tasting and useful apples. Some weren't. Since apple seeds do not always produce apples that look like the parent trees, each apple along a trail could be a different kind.

By the time of John's death in March of 1845, at age seventy, he had become the Johnny Appleseed legend you read about today. An early biographer, Rosella Rice, met him when she was a child. She later wrote, "He . . . wore his hair and beard long and dressed oddly." Rice described Johnny as "good, kind, generous," and stated that all the orchards in the white settlements came from Johnny's nurseries.

Avocados are native to the West Indies and Central America. Archaeologists have found avocado seeds in Mexico that are thousands of years old. Mexico today is the largest grower of avocados for sale throughout the world. The avocado's Mexican name is *aguacate.*

Avocados first came to North America in 1833. A Mr. Henry Perrine planted them in Florida. The United States is now the second largest avocado grower in the world.

Avocados grow on trees. Other names for the avocado are avocado pear, because of the fruit's shape, and alligator pear, because of its slightly rough skin. Size varies from 8 ounces (230 grams) to 3 pounds (1.4 kilograms). An avocado has more protein than any other fruit. It contains vitamin A and several B vitamins. It also contains about 25 percent fat.

In some places, an avocado's creamy yellowish insides are mashed and spread on bread, like butter or peanut butter. This makes a healthy sandwich. Occasionally it is called *midshipman's butter*, because it stored better than butter on ships. Try a mashed avocado sandwich sometime.

Avocado
Persea americana

Bean
Phaseolus species

All kinds of beans date back to prehistoric times. Bean seeds have been found in archaeological digs in both South America and Mexico. By the time of the Spanish conquests, beginning in 1519, records show the Aztec emperor Montezuma taking in 5,000 tons of beans a year as tribute from his many subjects.

The padres, or priests, accompanying Spanish adventurers carried kidney beans to Europe in the 1500s. People called them *Indian beans*. But they weren't grown as a food crop. Bean vines were grown for their pretty flowers. After a while, people started to eat beans. Soon beans became a basic part of food cooking.

Europeans also tried eating roasted beans as a medicine to cure the dreaded smallpox. As with many other long-ago "cures," this didn't work, and millions died.

Across the ocean, Native American Indians also used kidney beans, along with corn and squash. They had been growing them since before recorded time. Kidney beans were called *ogaressa* by the Hurons, *mushaquissedes* by the Pequods, and *malachxil* by the Delawares. Indians planted beans of varying colors in each corn hill. As the vines grew, they used the cornstalks for support.

Prehistoric Indians had learned to domesticate the wild tepary bean that grew in canyons. They called it *pawi*. Pawi grew where little else would in extremely dry areas. The southwestern Papagos ate, by necessity, so much pawi, they were called the "bean people."

When Spanish explorers arrived, they asked the bean's name. The Papagos answered "t'pawi," which translates, "It is a bean." The Spanish heard this as "tepary," and the name still exists. Tepary beans come in varying colors, including dark brown, purplish black, and speckled yellow.

In 1796, an English doctor, Edward Jenner, discovered a vaccination that prevented smallpox.

There were several early superstitions about beans. If a person wanted to get rid of a ghost, one way was to spit beans at it. Also a person sleeping all night in a bean field was sure to wake up crazy. And farmers raising hens had to make certain the hens didn't eat beans. If they did, the hens wouldn't lay eggs.

Among the Zunis, the colors were used in specific ceremonies. Young boys, initiated into one of six Zuni kivas (like a men's club), had to bring a bowl of boiled tepary beans of the kiva's color to the ceremony.

Long before the Pilgrims arrived, Native American Indians grew hundreds of different kinds of beans. In areas where winters were long and cold, food could be quite difficult to find. But dried beans keep well for years if protected from animals and insects. New England Indian tribes dried beans, then soaked them in water when ready to use. One special dish mixed beans with maple sugar and bear fat. These beans were baked overnight.

Now there are over 1,000 different types of beans. They come in many colors, designs, and shapes. How many have you seen? Today there are bean festivals, where beans are seen that never appear in most city markets. This includes the Oregon giant bean which has 8-inch (20-centimeter) long pods with pale blue spots, and the Dalmatian bean, white with dark red spots.

Beans contain vitamin A, potassium, phosphorus, and iron, plus some B vitamins. The biggest grower of soybeans is the United States, and we supply most of the world, including China. China grows more fava beans, however, and Africa is the top grower of lima beans. Lima beans were named for Lima, Peru.

An early tongue twister was "Three blue beans in a blue bladder." Can you say this correctly three times in a row?

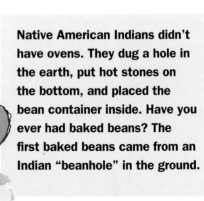

Native American Indians didn't have ovens. They dug a hole in the earth, put hot stones on the bottom, and placed the bean container inside. Have you ever had baked beans? The first baked beans came from an Indian "beanhole" in the ground.

Native American Bean Game

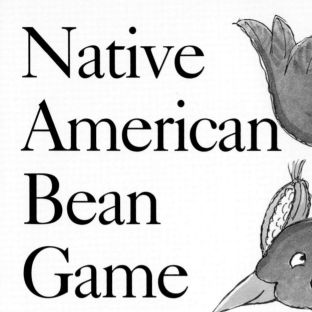

Would you like to play a south-western Indian tepary bean game?

Start with 10 white beans, 10 black beans, and 1 yellow bean (or as close as you can get to this). Get a gourd from the supermarket. If you can't find a gourd, you can play this game with a cup.

Player *A* puts 1 bean of each color into the hollow gourd, shakes it, then tosses the beans out. If the yellow bean falls nearer the black than the white, then *A* must give *B* both the black and white beans. If it falls closer to the white, then *B* must give *A* both the black and white beans. Then it is *B*'s turn. The winner is the one who gets all the beans first.

Bean Legend

According to many Indian legends, the Giver of Life sent the first corn (maize) and beans. In the Narragansett legend, a crow brought these necessary vegetables. The crow flew in carrying a grain of corn in one ear and a bean in the other. Because of this, no Narragansett Indian would ever bother a crow feeding in a corn patch.

The earliest carrots came from Afghanistan. They were purple and skinny, and had a branched shape. There may have been black and red carrots, too, but no orange or yellow.

Carrot seeds traveled to Asia Minor, then Spain, and on to Europe with the traveling Moors. Carrots became larger when the Greeks began cultivating them in private gardens. Tracing the carrot's early history isn't easy. Sometimes writers talked about carrots when they really meant parsnips, and vice versa.

In the 1700s, Dutch scientists bred the pale orange carrot. They worked with it until they had a bright orange carrot. Cooks liked this a lot better than the purple carrot that turned brown when cooked. So orange carrots were everyplace. Dutch botanists also got rid of the bitter taste of the original wild carrot.

Carrot
Daucus carota

When the Dutch sent boatloads of fruits and vegetables across the English Channel to feed the growing population of London, carrots came, too. At first, the English grew them for their lacy white flowers. Then they grew carrots for food and medicine. Carrot tea, made from dried leaves, was supposed to help people survive the pain of kidney stones.

Carrots, or "carrets," came to America with the earliest pioneers. This vegetable grew so well, it was used to feed livestock as well as people. When the colonists wanted their butter to have a nice healthy orange-yellow color, they added carrot juice to the butter churn.

Carrots have huge amounts of vitamin A. They also contain some calcium, phosphorus, and potassium. It's hard to think about eating too many carrots. But it is possible. Then you might turn yellow like the butter. But it goes away after you stop eating them.

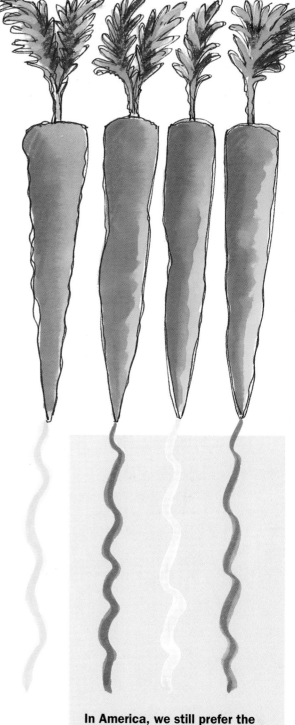

In America, we still prefer the orange carrot. But in Europe, orange, yellow, red, white, and purple varieties are commonly grown.

Carrots in Mythology

Perhaps you have heard about the famed Trojan horse? A story, maybe true, maybe not, talks about a war over Helen, a very pretty young queen, between the ancient Greek cities of Sparta and Troy. The war had been going on for ten years. Finally the Trojan soldiers seemed to have control over their city. But the warrior Ulysses thought of a way to sneak in.

Ulysses' soldiers built a huge wooden horse. Inside, the horse was hollow. Ulysses ordered some of his best soldiers to hide within the horse. Then he left the horse by the Trojan gates and pretended to sail away with his army.

The Trojans were suspicious. But there wasn't a sound from within the horse. The Spartan soldiers were, of course, very quiet. The soldiers had even been given carrots as a medicine to stop their stomachs from rumbling.

After a while, the gift horse was pushed inside Troy. Celebrations were held around it all day. But in the dark of night, the Greek soldiers of Sparta snuck out and captured Troy. Today, when some people are suspicious of gift givers, they use the phrase Trojan horse to refer to the gift.

Celery's ancestors grew at seaside marshes in the eastern Mediterranean area. Wild celery still grows there. Its companions are bulrushes and willows. These plants also prefer soggy soil. Wild celery is a low-growing herb. It doesn't look much like today's fancy leafed vegetable. The old form of celery also is quite bitter tasting.

Food gatherers didn't pay much attention to celery until Greek and Roman civilization began. Then, since it still tasted awful, celery was used more as a medicine than a food. Many believe the word *celery* comes from the Latin word *celer* meaning "quick acting."

The Romans ate celery to cure stomach problems and to encourage a good night's sleep. They also wove celery stalks and leaves together to make wreaths. If a person ate or drank too much, placing a celery wreath upon the head, like a hat, was supposed to make the person feel better.

Celery
Apium graveolens dulce

Celery was still used in Europe hundreds of years later to cure all sorts of stomach problems. During the early Middle Ages (A.D. 500–1050) celery was one of the medicines given to people bitten by wild dogs. They hoped it would make them feel better. But celery wasn't all serious. On the entertainment front, magicians put celery seeds in their shoes. This was supposed to help them fly. If they did, it was due to some other trick.

After A.D. 1050, most Europeans seemed to stop using celery for any reason. It showed up again in French garden planting lists about the 1500s. Its name is *celeri* in French, *Selleri* in Denmark, *sedano* in Italy, and *Sellerie* in German. By now it was much pleasanter tasting.

The American colonists brought "celary" seed with them to plant in the New World. But celery never grew well for them. It was, and still is, fussy about its soil and water. It took another 200 years before celery was grown enough to become popular. Today people eat it plain as a crunchy diet food, or with peanut butter or cream cheese as a snack.

Celery contains some vitamin A, potassium, and phosphorus, but not much. A stalk is 94 percent water. If you have a juicer at home, you can try making celery juice.

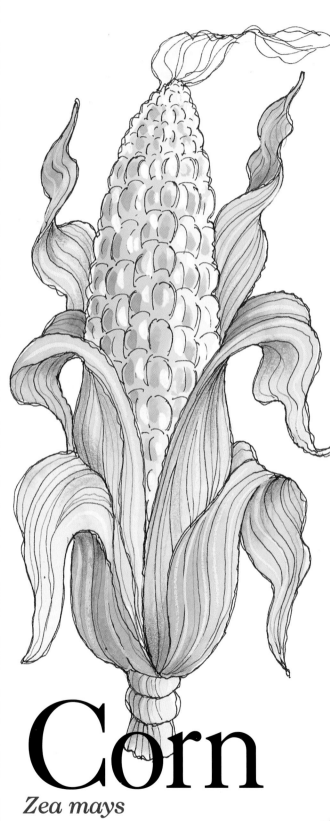

Corn
Zea mays

Wild corn, which no longer exists today, dates back to at least 7000 B.C. in Central America. People living in rock shelters gathered it for food. They used stone cooking pots. The pot was kept in the center of the fire area. It was very heavy, so a new stone pot was made each time the group moved to a different cave.

Cultivated, or deliberately grown, Indian corn, called *maize*, dates back to at least 5000 B.C. The oldest corn fossils come from Mexico. They were only about 1/2 inch (1.3 centimeters) long.

Maize kernels were removed from the cob and dried to make them last longer. When needed for food, they were boiled with a little lime or charcoal added to the water. The addition of lime provided niacin, one of the important B vitamins. This was before anyone knew about vitamins. Countries that used maize for food but did not use the lime cooking method, had people with pellagra, a severe niacin deficiency disorder.

After boiling, the maize kernels were rubbed between hands to remove the maize skin. Then kernels were crushed with a stone roller to form a paste. The paste or dough was kneaded and made into thin round cakes, or what we know as tortillas.

From Aztec times on, maize, beans, tomatoes, and a special hot pepper were food staples in Mexico. Maize porridge with honey or spiced with red pepper might be part of breakfast. Lunch could be maize tortillas, with beans of many varieties and a sauce of tomatoes and peppers.

From Mexico, maize traveled to South America, reaching there about 3000 B.C. Wandering tribes brought it to North America. Here, Native American Indians grew maize or corn long before any European explorer noticed the New World. They gathered maize ears, not removing the husks. The maize ears were covered with mud, then roasted in hot fire embers. Some ears were dried and saved for winter eating.

Ripe corn was pounded into a meal, then dried or parched to make a form of flour. Ground cornmeal was also used to make puddings, to which grasshoppers and blueberries were sometimes added for protein, vitamins, and flavor.

Columbus first saw *mahiz* growing in the West Indies. He referred to it as "a sort of grain called *maiz*." He noticed that it was "most tasty, boiled, roasted, or ground into flour." In 1493, he carried maize or corn seeds home to Spain. (*Corn* was an all-purpose name for any type of grain.) Corn was immediately popular and soon was grown in far-off places like China, Africa, India, and the Philippines.

Native American Algonquian Indian tribes taught the first French and English settlers how to plant several types of corn. Without the corn obtained from the Indians, early settlers would have starved before they could have planted and harvested their own.

The Pilgrims were introduced to popcorn at their first Thanksgiving feast in 1621. Chief Massasoit of the Wampanoag tribe brought "parched corn" in a deerskin bag as an after dinner treat.

The earliest method of popping
corn was to toss kernels into
the embers of a fire. Soon
popped corn was a popular settler breakfast food, eaten with
milk and maple sugar. Why
don't you try this for breakfast
sometime?

Popping corn is a special type of corn. The corn kernels are very hard. There is a small amount of moisture inside each kernel. When heated, any moisture inside turns to steam. As the cooking temperature gets near the boiling point, pressure builds up inside the small kernel. Popping comes about when the soft watery starch inside the kernel expands enough to explode the kernel, turning it inside out.

Learning from the Indians, the colonists soon grew corn of all kinds and colors, including purple, orange, and blue. The many-colored corn often seen around Thanksgiving for decorations is usually called *Indian corn*.

The colonists ground corn into meal in several ways. One way was by putting corn kernels into a hollow tree stump and pounding the kernels with a heavy log. Can you grind corn in your classroom? Is it easy to do? Young boys were often given this job in pioneer days.

No part of the corn, cob, or leaves were wasted by thrifty pioneers. Mothers made corncob dolls for the children, designing dresses and hats with cloth scraps and painting on faces. Corn silk was used for the doll's hair.

Pictures from those days show men smoking corncob pipes. Both men and boys wore hats woven from corn husks. Leaves or husks could make up a mattress. It is said that President Abraham Lincoln, noted for his poor beginning in life, was born on a bed of cornhusks.

Corn was even used for contests. During harvest time, the many corn ears were placed in big equal piles. Teams competed to see which would be the first to husk, or take the leaves off, all the corn in their pile.

Early pioneers often used corn as money. They paid the blacksmith with corn ears or cornmeal, and also paid their rent and taxes with it.

The United States grows the most corn of anyplace in the world, with the leading producers being Iowa and Illinois. China is second in world production, and Brazil is third. In the United States, most corn is used at home. About half goes to feed cattle, sheep, chickens, and hogs. But we do get lots of it in cornmeal for tortillas, cornflakes, corn bread, corn syrup, and corn oil. Little is wasted. Corn, or its cob, in some form or another is found in chewing gum, ketchup, paste, cough syrup, soap, crayons, marshmallows, plastic, and pancake mix.

Corn Legends

The beginning of corn was a part of many tribal legends. For example, the Navajo Indians believed that corn began when a magic turkey was carrying corn ears to the morning star and dropped one along the way.

Corn color had its own history in the Tewa tribe of New Mexico. Long ago, the people ate mostly meat, the story goes. But then forest fires killed all the animals. The people were starving. The Indians went to a sacred place and danced for many weeks while the elders waited for guidance from the gods.

They finally had a dream that six pebbles of different colors should be placed in a small hole. This hole should be covered with a stone. After doing this, the people danced again. When they looked in the hole, six corn plants of different colors had sprouted. From this come the six different colors of corn.

Maize, or corn, was a very important part of the spiritual life of many Native American tribes. It had many names, including Giver of Life and Seed of Seeds.

There were special planting and harvesting ceremonies. For example, Cibecue Apache women selected the seed to be planted. As the corn went into the ground, a woman would speak to it, telling it to "grow fast." When corn tassles formed, the woman in charge of that particular ritual would go into the field and sing, "Make a good ear."

Each May, the kachina ceremonial dancers of the Hopi Indians wore masks painted like rainbows for their ceremonial corn planting dances. They sang a special song about butterflies and bees flying over the cornfields. The butterflies "with pollen painted faces, chase one another . . ."

All tribes had religious festivals of thanksgiving when corn was harvested.

All grapes are not the same. There are table grapes that are eaten fresh, raisin grapes, juice grapes, and grapes used to make wine. Grapes can be purple, green, black, blue, golden, red, or white. How many colors can you find in the market?

Grapes are among the oldest of cultivated plants. The Bible contains about 200 references to grapes, beginning with Noah planting a vineyard. The Hebrew word is *gefen*. Egyptians grew grapes 6,000 years ago. Pictures of grapes were painted on the sides of Egyptian tombs dating to 2440 B.C.

To make raisins, people buried fresh grapes in the hot desert sand. Drying removes water, but not natural sugar. The result was a wrinkly sweet grape. Grape sugar was also made long ago. Grape juice was squeezed out and left to evaporate until the sugar remained. This sugar was very important. Aside from honey, there was no other form of sweetening.

Grapes are mentioned in the oldest known written language, Sumarian, in script dating back to about 3000 B.C.

Grape

Vitis

Native American Indians grew grapes as far back as 1800 B.C. Native American Indians used grapes in many ways besides as fresh fruit and juice. Grapes were dried as winter fruit. Grape leaves were used as a medicine. Grape leaves were tied around the head of a person with headaches. Soaked in water, grape leaves were put on top of wounds to speed healing.

Early North American settlers mentioned that there were at least 40 different types of grapes growing when they arrived. Martha's Vineyard in Massachusetts was named by an English explorer who found grape fields there when he landed.

Grapes have some vitamin C, which the settlers used to prevent scurvy. Grapes also contain vitamin A and some potassium.

Now there are about 8,000 grape varieties. Ninety-two percent of fresh-eating, or table grapes, come from California. Spain and California are the leading raisin growers.

When Viking explorers came to America about the year A.D. 1006, they found grapes growing. They called this newly "discovered" land *Vinland* because of the grapes.

25

The story of edible lettuce begins before recorded history. There was possibly a wild lettuce parent. Cultivation probably began in the Mediterranean area about 3,000 years ago.

Early lettuce did not look like today's tightly bunched varieties. Early lettuce had a tall central stalk, with leaves coming out of that stalk. Persian kings served loose leaf lettuce on royal tables as early as 550 B.C. They called it *kahn*. The Greeks grew it in their gardens as early as 500 B.C. They used it only during special festivals or for funeral feasts. To have lettuce present was considered a special honor.

Lettuce
Lactuca sativa

The ancient Greeks had an annual festival, one of many festivals, dedicated to Adonis, the handsome boyfriend of the goddess Aphrodite. For the festival feast, the Greeks grew lettuce and the herb fennel in green jars. They displayed these jars throughout the house, just like we display holiday flowers. The day after the festival, the jars were thrown away. After a while, anything that didn't last very long was called an *Adonis Garden*.

When Roman soldiers occupied England, they brought lettuce seeds with them. After 500 years, the Romans left, but lettuce remained and thrived. It was used mostly as an herbal medicine. Medical guides of the time suggested eating lettuce to cure heartburn and headaches, and drinking lettuce juice when you needed to calm down. It was also supposed to help ensure a good night's sleep. Have you ever seen the milky juice in lettuce stems? Take a look.

Lettuce is 95 percent water.

Lettuce arrived in France in the 1300s. Our name "lettuce" comes from the old French word *laitues*. This means *milky*. Wealthy French people served salads composed of four types of lettuce, pink and red rose petals, violet petals, mint leaves, sage leaves, and orange calendula petals. This colorful mix was drizzled with oil and vinegar dressing, much like our basic salad dressing today.

Columbus brought lettuce to the Americas, planting it in the West Indies in 1493. Early French, Dutch, Swedish, and English explorers took "lettice" seeds along with them. The early American colonists used dried lettuce tea to help them snooze. It was also supposed to be useful for stomach "wamblings" and scorpion bites, and to stop the itch of poison ivy.

In a sixteenth-century cookbook, the writer talks about salads, saying, "All sortes of Lettice are spent in sallets, while they are fresh and greene." Do you recognize all the words as words we use today in a different form?

Lettuce contains some vitamin A and some potassium. Today we eat many types of lettuce many different ways. How much of it? Thirty pounds a year per person. Most of America's lettuce is grown in California.

The history of onions goes back before recorded time. Nobody is really sure where they first grew. Many experts think it was southwestern Asia.

By 3000 B.C., several types of onions were grown in gardens. Writing on an ancient Egyptian pyramid wall complained about how expensive it was to provide slave workers with food onions and garlic. Other records mention that some Egyptian priests thought the roundness of an onion was a symbol of the whole universe. The onion layers, one on top of the other, seemed to copy the layers of heaven, earth, and a hell.

Wandering early tribes located onions by their special smell and used the bulb for food.

Onion
Allium cepa

29

Egyptian royalty had a very high opinion of onions. There were more pictures of onions on their pyramid tombs than of any other plant. There were always baskets of onions, among other foods such as bread, left within these burial sites for possible use after death. And if you ever wondered what was used to stuff an Egyptian mummy: onions and sawdust, among other items.

An old Turkish legend says the strong odor of onions dates back to when Satan was thrown out of heaven. Onions grew where he put his right foot, smelly garlic where he put his left.

Onions have quite an aroma. This is due to an oil within the plant. When onions are peeled or cut, the oil escapes into the air as an irritating vapor. That's what makes eyes tear.

The stronger the odor of the onion, the more power early people thought it had. A hearty Roman breakfast was raw onions on bread. Roman gladiators were rubbed with onion juice to make them strong. Greeks in training for early Olympic races were told to eat two onions a day to give them speed.

The Roman name for onion was *unio*. The onion was one bulb united instead of the separate bulbs found in garlic. The early French made *unio* into *ognon*, later *oignon*, and recently *ognon* again. The British word started out as *onyon*. From this came our present *onion*.

Medical uses for onions were many, from early times on. Because of an onion's roundness, people first thought that was nature's way of saying its juice was good for anything wrong with the head. That included deafness, eye problems, baldness, and slow thinking. Later its uses were expanded to other disorders, including dog bites, blisters, gunshot wounds, sleeplessness, pneumonia, and diabetes.

In more modern times, some people think onions cure high blood pressure. Research into the medical helpfulness of onions and garlic is still going on. Onions do contain a substance called *allylaldehyde*, which can help destroy some bacteria.

Wild onions, or meadow onions, grew in North America long before any early settlers arrived. Native American Indians ate wild onions raw after dipping them in salted water. They also dried the wild onion for food use during the long winters.

The first big yellow round onions came over on the Mayflower in 1620. Few colonial gardens were without them. Our first president, George Washington, said they were his favorite food. American cowboys in the wild west liked them too. Onions went into their campfire stew. The cowboy nickname for the smelly onion was *skunk eggs*.

An area along Lake Michigan had so many onions growing, Native American Indians there called it *Chicago*, referring to the smell.

Scientists estimate that orange ancestors date back about 20 million years. Some scientists believe oranges, lemons, and limes all began on one tree type, rather than three different tree types. Over thousands of years, the fruit became genetically different.

By 2400 B.C., Chinese scholars mentioned oranges in their written works. Because an orange's golden color made them seem quite valuable, rich people in China bought more oranges than anyone else. However, early oranges were used mostly for display since they tasted quite bitter.

Oranges made their way to India at least 2,000 years ago. The Hindu word for an orange was *naranga*, which may have meant "fragrance."

Orange

Citrus sinensis

In tenth-century Spain, oranges were considered so valuable and special, they were guarded carefully. Any stranger who dared eat, or even touch, a decorative orange in someone's garden risked being put to death.

The ongoing orange voyage never stopped. Their popularity traveled to Egypt and Iran, where the Persian word for them was *narang*. Then oranges crossed the Mediterranean Sea to Rome. As these pretty fruits traveled, their name changed. It became *naranja* in Spain and *orange* in France.

Oranges in early Europe weren't peeled and eaten. They still tasted fairly bitter. However, oranges were popular as a seasoning to give food a special flavor. Orange juice might be poured over roast chestnuts. Sometimes oranges were fried with cinnamon and sugar. The more important a guest was, the more golden oranges were put on the table for decoration or used in recipes.

It wasn't until 1616 that anyone in Europe ever tasted a sweet orange. At that time they were brought in by the Dutch East India Company from China. They were a big hit immediately. Just owning a sweet orange tree became a status symbol in England.

There is some argument over who first brought oranges to North America. It is most generally believed to be the Spanish explorer Hernando de Soto, who planted oranges where he camped in Florida. All oranges planted by the early explorers were bitter oranges.

Native American Indians brought seeds away from the Florida colonies. They scattered them in the surrounding wilderness. Sometimes a grove of orange trees along lakes and rivers gives modern searchers a clue to the location of long-ago Indian settlements.

From their very beginning, oranges were considered to be a health food. Drinking powdered orange peel in hot water was supposed to get rid of tapeworms. People believed carrying an orange around with them stopped or would cure the bubonic plague, another dreaded disease.

Oranges do promote good health, even though they don't get rid of parasites or infectious illnesses. Oranges contain vitamins C, A, and B, plus some calcium and phosphorus.

How many oranges have you eaten this week? In the United States, each person peels about $12\frac{1}{2}$ pounds (5.6 kilograms) of oranges per year.

The first oranges in California came with Father Junipero Serra and his Franciscan monks in 1769. As they established a chain of religious missions, they planted oranges. Now California and Florida are the main orange growing states.

Citrus and Scurvy: The Seafarer's Rescue Food

Oranges and other citrus fruits helped prevent the dreaded scurvy disease that killed many seamen on long-distance voyages before 1774.

Back when traveling between Europe and America could take eight months by sea, the voyage was not only slow but dangerous. Sailors often didn't get a good diet. They ate what could be dried out enough not to spoil on ship. But tough salted meat, dried peas, and hard insect-infested biscuits don't offer much in the way of vitamin C. Vitamin C is important for healthy gums, hair, teeth, skin, and bones.

Without vitamin C, the sailors bruised easily. Their hair fell out. So did their teeth. Bones broke easily. Muscles always hurt. Sores grew on arms and legs. If sailors went long enough without vitamin C in their food, they died. On some exploration sea voyages, almost half the sailors died from scurvy alone.

Then, in 1756, John Lind, a doctor in the British navy, discovered that sailors who drank lemon or orange juice, or who ate fresh fruit everyday, never became ill from scurvy. But all that fancy food cost money. Oranges and lemons also used up valuable ship space. Sea captains didn't want to carry them on board. Scurvy continued to kill more seamen than the battles they got into with enemy ships.

It wasn't until 16 years later that attitudes changed. Captain Cook did a three-year trip around the world. Cook kept his sailors healthy by putting fresh fruit on board at each stop. Not one of his sailors got the dreaded scurvy. By 1774, almost all ships carried oranges, lemons, limes, or lime juice as part of the food ration. The British word for sailor became "limey."

In ancient Greek and Roman times, fried peas were sold at circuses, much like we sell popcorn today.

Pea
Pisum sativum

The oldest discovery of peas was in a cave, called the Spirit Cave, on the border between Burma and Thailand. These peas date back to about 9750 B.C. Cave dwellers in Asia and Europe probably ate some form of pea seeds. Scientists who study prehistoric times seem to think these pea seeds were larger and tougher than our current peas. To make them softer and easier to eat, cave dwellers probably peeled the seeds, then roasted them over a fire.

Peas served several food purposes in ancient Greek and Roman times. Without refrigerators, meat was heavily salted to preserve it, like jerky. But people didn't like the taste of all that salt. So peas were put in the meat cook pots as salt blotters. Poor people, who couldn't afford meat, ate peas with their cereal.

The first peas in England arrived with French Norman soldiers about A.D. 1066. Peas soon grew in monastery gardens. The original Latin word was *pisum*. This became *peason*. After a while "peason" became simply "pease," and later plain "peas."

Dried peas were a basic foodstuff on the many exploring sea voyages of the time.

The small wooden ships absorbed sea water. No food could be kept dry for very long, and so any fresh food spoiled quickly. So peas, dried salted beef or pork, and dried bread or biscuits were often all the sailors had to eat for months on end.

Columbus's ships brought peas to the New World in 1493. They were among the earliest crops planted in the Americas. "We put some of our Peaze in the grounde," wrote a colonist in 1584. Later all settlers grew "pease" if the climate permitted.

Dried peas have a very good storage life. They protected against hunger during the long, cold winters. The dried peas were soaked or boiled. Peas were served in wheat cereal, or porridge, for a hearty breakfast. It could be hot cereal or cold cereal. And this cereal could sit in the pot for quite a while without spoiling. Do you remember the clapping rhyme "Pease porridge hot, pease porridge cold, pease porridge in the pot, nine days old"? Your parents or grandparents might have heard it from their parents, too. Ask them.

Ships' biscuits were made from flour and water. They were so hard, it was like biting into a brick. Bread and peas became infested with insect larvae or worms. They still had to be eaten for there was nothing else. The meat was so tough that what the sailors couldn't eat they carved into snuffboxes and trinkets.

While colonists and sailors were eating dried peas, the French were enjoying the fad of fresh peas. If you were rich enough, you could afford as many as you wanted. One royal court lady in France wrote that eating, enjoying, and thinking about fresh peas was so important, the royal princes talked about peas for "four days." Some royal court ladies not only ate peas at the royal table, but ate them before going to bed. "It is both a fashion and a madness," said the royal writer.

But not far away, in 1600s England, fresh peas were thought of as a food for poor people only. One rather snobby writer said it was a rather "frightful thing" to see people buying and eating peas.

There are several early English-Scottish superstitions about peas. One superstition is that if a young unmarried woman is shelling peas and finds nine in one pod, she is certain to marry. Another superstition is that if she places the pea pod with the nine peas over the door, she will marry the first man who enters.

Have you ever shelled peas? Try it. How many are in a normal pod?

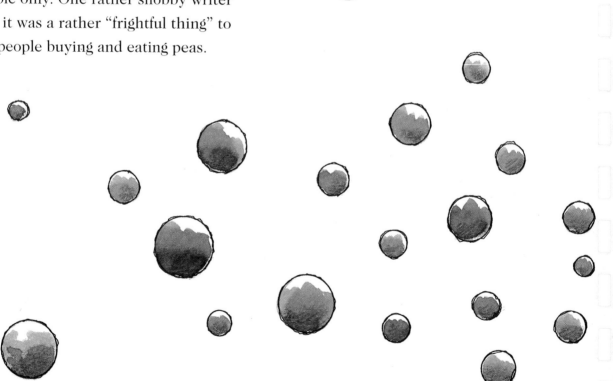

Pea Mythology

There is a Norse, or Viking, myth about the beginning of the pea. The thunder god, Thor, was in a bad mood. He sent a group of dragons flying through the air. They carried peas. The dragons were to drop the peas in people's water wells as punishment for angering Thor. When the peas filled up the wells and started rotting, the people wouldn't have any more water.

On the journey, the dragons accidentally dropped some of the peas on the ground. They started to grow. This is how peas on earth began, or so the story was told in about the year A.D. 800.

39

Did you know the nectarine is a smooth-skinned peach?

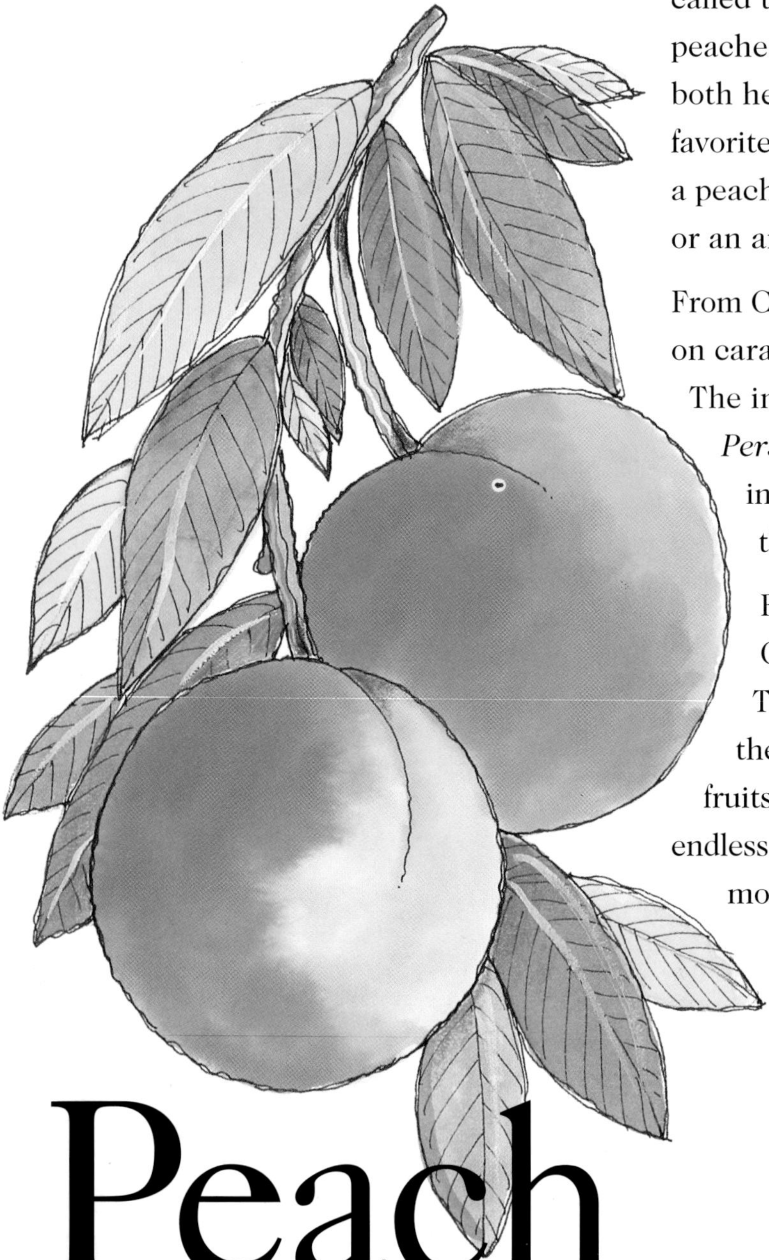

Peach trees are believed to have originated in China at least 4,000 years ago. Ancient Chinese writers called them "the tree of life." Having peaches in a home was supposed to bring both health and long life. If you had a favorite friend, you would give that person a peach. This could be either a real peach or an artificial one designed by an artist.

From China, peach stones, or pits, traveled on caravans to India and then to Persia. The invading Romans called peaches *Persian apples*, and wrote about them in A.D. 79. Early peaches were smaller than those we know now.

From Persia, the peach traveled to Greece with the Roman armies. Then Roman conquerors brought the peach to Great Britain. Like many fruits, the peach was saved from the endless wars of the time by the efforts of monks, who cultivated them safely behind monastery walls.

Peach

Prunus persica

In some places in China today, a birthday dish—a steamed roll shaped like a peach—called *shou-tao,* is still offered. This means "long life peach."

When Spanish explorers began their adventures into the New World, they took peaches with them. In 1565, the Spanish planted the first peach orchards in St. Augustine, Florida, their first colony. Later, French, English, and Dutch settlers began planting peaches.

Native American Indians, including the Creek, Cherokee, Natchez, and Seminole tribes enjoyed this new fruit. They carried the stones westward, planting them around campsites and long trails. The pits went from one tribe to another, until most tribes that could grow them, did.

Peaches contain a lot of vitamin A, plus phosphorus, potassium, protein, and vitamin C. There are now about 300 peach varieties grown in North America. The United States has over 30 million peach trees, more than all other countries combined. California is the main peach growing state.

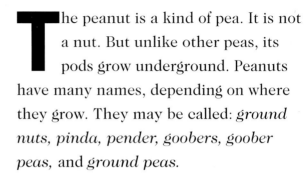

The peanut is a kind of pea. It is not a nut. But unlike other peas, its pods grow underground. Peanuts have many names, depending on where they grow. They may be called: *ground nuts, pinda, pender, goobers, goober peas,* and *ground peas.*

The peanut's first home was in Central and South America. The Maya Indians of the Yucatan grew them, as did the Inca of Peru, who called it *anchic.* Scientists have found jars with peanut designs in Peruvian tombs more than 1,500 years old. When Spanish soldiers and adventurers arrived looking for gold, they carried peanuts home, too.

Peanut
Arachis hypogaea

Peanuts traveled to Brazil, then to Portugal. The Portuguese began peanut growing in Africa as a cheap and nourishing crop to feed captive workers. When their slave ships began collecting Africans to work in colonial Virginia tobacco and cotton fields, another part of the cargo was peanuts. Peanuts didn't spoil easily and they were full of protein and vitamins. They became a basic part of the shipboard diet for the captured humans transported on the boats.

It is also believed by many researchers that the captured Africans brought peanuts along themselves. They did not know what was going to happen to them or whether they would receive food. The African word for peanuts was *nguba*. It later became *goober*, a word still used today in the South, a goober pea.

Until the Civil War, peanuts, which grow best in hot summer areas, were strictly a southern food item. Few people in the northern states even knew about them. What happened?

Hungry Union soldiers fighting in the South had gotten used to eating camp-fire roasted ground nuts as part of their meals. When the Civil War ended, the soldiers went home to more fun things—like baseball. Every Saturday and

Sunday, crowds would gather in special parks to cheer a favorite team.

People cheering a team liked a snack, just like today. The former soldiers remembered the great ground nuts they had eaten in the South. Somebody got the idea of ordering peanuts, roasting them, and selling them at baseball games. The popularity of the nutritious peanut spread from here to many different uses.

In 1895, Dr. John Harvey Kellogg was thinking of healthy foods that patients with bad teeth could eat without having pain. He suggested to his brother Will Keith Kellogg, who ran a sanitarium, or nursing home, that Will experiment with peanuts. Peanuts are very high in protein. They contain 30 percent protein, plus calcium, phosphorus, potassium, and B vitamins.

"I bought ten pounds of peanuts," W. K. Kellogg recalled, "roasted them in the oven a little while, put them in a pillowcase to remove the hulls, winnowed out the husks, put the material through the rolls [used for making their wheat flakes] and made the first peanut butter. I took it to Dr. Kellogg and he named it . . ." Maybe the name *Kellogg* rings a bell. The brothers invented Kellogg's breakfast cereals.

Today, most peanuts are grown in the warmer areas of Africa, India, and Asia. There peanut butter is used to thicken sauces and soups. Only in Australia and America is peanut butter regularly used on bread.

American southern states grow a lot of peanuts. They have many uses. By squashing the nuts, manufacturers get

oil. Peanuts contain about 40 to 50 percent oil. This oil may be used in soap, shaving cream, margarine, plastic, shampoo, paint, and salad oil, and around canned sardines. Peanut oil can be used to oil machinery, too.

Peanut Story: George Washington Carver

When anyone talks about peanut history, you'll always hear the name George Washington Carver. Born in Missouri about 1864, toward the end of the Civil War, his parents were slaves. They both died when he was a baby. George was raised by the Carver family who had owned his mother, Mary.

George was a sickly child and couldn't do heavy work. Instead, he helped around the farmhouse and tended the family garden. Even as a youngster, he was always very interested in plants. He had a little garden of his own, and became known around the area as "the plant doctor."

The Carvers, who had no children of their own, realized George was very intelligent. They hired a private tutor for him. Afterward, George went to a local school. But he soon had more questions than the teacher could answer. At age fourteen, George left for Kansas, determined to get an education.

Adopting the name George Washington Carver, he later worked his way through Iowa State College in an endless series of difficult and odd jobs. Graduating in 1894, he became an assistant botanist at Iowa State College. In 1896, after obtaining a master's degree in agriculture, he joined the staff of Tuskegee Institute in Alabama. George went on to become a chemist with a special interest in agricultural research.

George Washington Carver researched many plants, including the sweet potato, sugar beet, and pecan. He found more than 300 uses for peanuts. These included: coffee made from peanuts, peanut milk, chocolate covered peanuts, dyes made from peanut skins, peanut oil face cream and peanut oil massage cream, several types of peanut butter, peanut soup, peanut ice cream, and peanut flour bread.

By the end of World War I, the beginning peanut industry was worth $80 million. Carver's research made southern agriculture successful after the cotton crops failed because of boll weevil infestations.

Carver died in 1943. There is now a George Washington Carver National Monument on the Missouri farm where he was born. January 5 is George Washington Carver Day.

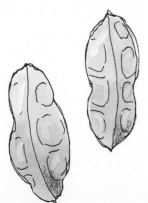

The potato started out as an ugly duckling vegetable some 10,000 years ago. It was small, about walnut size, and full of lumps and bumps. But the powerful Inca Indians of Peru prized it as food. It was very difficult to grow things in the high, cold Andes mountains. But the hardy potato plants survived.

A potato is about 78 percent water. Part of every crop was set out overnight in the chill air. The next morning, Inca servants spread out the partially frozen potatoes, then began stamping on them. This was done about four days in a row. When the water was all stamped out, the flattened blackened potato was dried and stored. These dried potatoes, known as *chuno*, lasted a very long time in storage.

From this early "freeze-dried" potato, the Inca made a form of flour, used for bread and other cooking. The Inca thought potatoes were so important, they made pots shaped like potatoes, and whistles, too. They even buried their dead with potatoes for snacks, just in case.

Potato
Solanum tuberosum

The potato is actually a part of an underground stem specialized for plant food storage. It has the fancy name *tuber*. When a group of Spanish explorers, led by Francisco Pizzaro, discovered the Inca culture about 1553, they also discovered the potato. They called it by the native name for the sweet potato: *batata*. They wrongfully thought this white potato was another form of sweet potato.

Pizzaro carried some batatas, or potatoes, back home. They weren't well received. "Anything that looks like that, with bumps and lumps, must carry disease," was the general thought. Back then, before microscopes let people look at bacteria and viruses, all sorts of strange things were thought to cause illness.

Seafaring adventurer Sir Francis Drake first brought potatoes to British notice in 1585. Drake had picked up food supplies in Central America for the journey home. Potatoes were among the supplies.

Drake stopped his ships to give some potatoes to starving settlers in Roanoke, an early Virginia colony set up by Sir Walter Raleigh. Raleigh, another swash-buckler of the time, grew them, and, in turn, gave some as a gift to Queen Elizabeth I.

The poor potato. The royal cooks took one look at its lumps and bumps and decided that couldn't be the portion any-one would want to eat. So they threw the tuber out, and served the stems and leaves instead.

Potatoes are related to tomatoes and egg-plant and to the poisonous nightshade plant. Healthy tubers don't bother any-body. Quite the contrary. They contain calcium, phosphorus, and potassium in addition to vitamin C. But eating the leaves will make a person sick. So every-body at the queen's dinner table that evening got horribly ill. Potatoes were banned from court for several hundred years.

Sir Walter Raleigh had a home in Ireland, too. He planted some potatoes there. They grew well. By the early 1700s, potatoes had become a main food in Ireland. Just 1¹/₂ acres of potatoes would feed a poor Irish farmer's family of six for a year.

Where there were too many people for too little available land, this was good news. Soon the poor grew and ate little else. Each person ate about 10 pounds (4.5 kilograms) of potatoes a day, accompanied by oatmeal and salt herring. The farmers also fed cattle and hogs on the potato scraps.

There now is an international potato center near Lima, Peru. It has over 5,000 potato types in its collection.

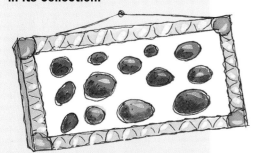

Many more potato varieties were available in the early 1900s. But because some travel better than others, or sell better, fewer varieties are grown today.

Then a potato fungus struck in 1845. It was called the black rot, because it turned potatoes black. They rotted quickly in the field. Although there had been potato problems before, this time the entire Irish potato crop was ruined. Within three years, more than 1 million people died of hunger, and another million left Ireland. Many people came to the United States. Since then, scientists have worked very hard developing potatoes resistant to this fungus.

The beautiful potatoes we eat today didn't come about until 1873, when Luther Burbank began working with them. He developed the Russet Burbank. The name is unfamiliar, perhaps. But some fast food restaurants use this for their french fries.

More than 100 potato varieties are available to the public, some only in farmers' markets. Over 300 million tons of potatoes are grown each year. In the United States, Idaho grows the most potatoes. Next time you go to the grocery store, see how many different types you can find.

Potato Chips

Potato chips were invented in the late 1800s in America by a Native American Indian, George Crum. He was a chef at a famous New York hotel. A customer told him that the fried potatoes being served weren't any good. They were too thick.

Tired of the complaints, Crum decided to slice the potatoes almost paper thin. He then fried them. They turned out crispy. Surprisingly, the fussy customer liked them, and so did the rest of the world.

The word *pumpkin* evolved from the Greek word *pepon*. This later became the French word *popon*. The American word went from *pompion* and *pumpion* to *pumpkin*.

The pumpkin is related to squash, cucumbers, and cantaloupes. Its ancestors can be traced to Mexico and go back at least 9,000 years. The early written history of pumpkins is quite confusing. Pumpkins were also called *melons* and *gourds*. Because there were melons and gourds that were not pumpkins, historians are not always certain to what the writer is referring.

It is known that American Indian tribes grew pumpkins for food long before any European explorers arrived. Columbus carried pumpkin seeds on his return trips to Europe, but the resulting melons weren't enjoyed. The grown melons were used to feed pigs.

Pumpkin
Cucurbita maxima

The early New England settlers weren't great pumpkin fans either. But during their first cold, long winter, when food was very scarce, they changed their minds. A common cooking method was to let a fire die down, then place a whole pumpkin in the ashes. When baked soft, the pumpkin was cut open. Honey or maple syrup was poured on top, and so was animal fat.

Pumpkin pie was another recipe. But it didn't look like the pies today. The Pilgrims cut off the pumpkin top.

They scraped out the seeds. Inside the hole went apples, sugar, spices, and milk. With the top back on again, the pumpkin was baked in the fire ashes.

Originally pumpkins were small and bitter. Now they can be huge or so tiny they fit in an open hand. One modern contest-winning pumpkin weighed 750 pounds (340 kilograms) and was 12 feet (3.7 meters) around. Would that have been big enough for Cinderella's coach?

Pumpkin Seed Snacks

1 Wash the seeds clean.

2 Dry the seeds.

3 Lightly oil a cookie sheet.

4 Sprinkle the seeds on the cookie sheet (only a single layer, no clumps).

5 Lightly salt the seeds, if you like salt.

6 Bake the seeds at 250°F (140°C) for about $\frac{1}{2}$ hour.

7 You may want an adult to stir the seeds a bit so they don't burn.

8 Cool the seeds, then eat them.

Apache Indian Pumpkin Seed Planting Ceremony

Just as the pumpkin vines started to show above ground, a small boy was sent out to collect juniper berries. On his return, a blindfold was placed over his eyes. The boy was then led to the pumpkin patch. Here he threw the berries in all directions. Wherever they landed, it was hoped many pumpkins would grow.

An Apache pumpkin seed planting ceremony was held every year in the spring. It was hoped this ceremony would result in a large pumpkin crop.

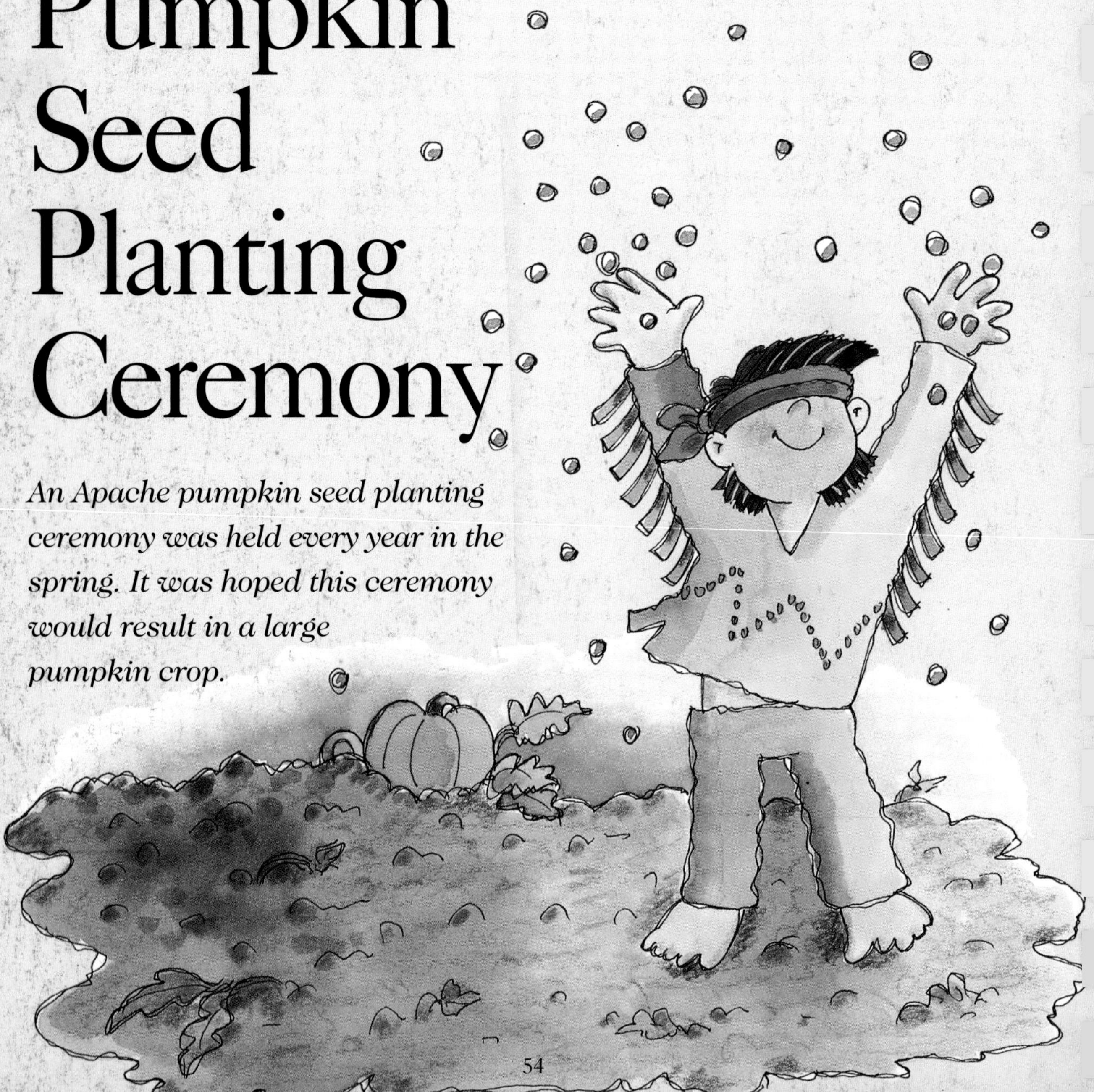

Halloween History

Nobody is positive about how today's Halloween started. It dates back at least 2,000 years. Most people think it is based on the ancient Celtic feast for the dead, called Samhain. *This feast began on October 31. This was the beginning of the Celtic New Year, a way of celebrating the autumn grain harvest, and also the beginning of winter.*

It was believed that on the night of October 31, the dead could come back and visit the living. The dead would come back in strange and terrifying forms.

As the Celtic religion declined and the Christian Church spread, the autumn harvest celebration changed form. November 1 became the Feast of All Saints or All Hallows. November 2 became the Feast of All Souls. On the evening of October 31, costumed children would go door to door begging for sweet soul cakes. In return, the givers would earn prayers for the dead. This trade-off was the beginning of tricks or treats on All Hallows Eve, or Hallowe'en.

When the Irish came to America in the 1800s, they brought the custom of All Hallows Eve with them. However, Halloween costuming gradually became more of a fun game. What's the strangest costume you have tried? What's the strangest costume you have seen?

What about pumpkins? Nobody ever thought to use pumpkins for Halloween at first. Pumpkins weren't grown in Europe. But large turnips were. So European children celebrating Halloween made their jack-o'-lanterns from large turnips. The turnips were carved much as we carve a Halloween pumpkin today. Inside the turnip, children placed a lit candle. The grinning wicked face was supposed to scare off ghosts.

American colonists grew more pumpkins than turnips. So the children changed the vegetable they used for Halloween. Thus, we have the pumpkin jack-o'-lantern.

Jack-O'-Lantern Myths

There are many stories about how the jack-o'-lanterns came about for Halloween. One Irish folktale told about a stingy man named Jack. Jack was so stingy, he was not allowed into heaven. Instead he was sent to hell. But he kept playing practical jokes on the devil. So he was thrown out of hell and told to walk the earth with his lantern until Judgment Day.

Another tale tells about a blacksmith named Jack. He made some quick money selling his soul to the devil. But when the devil came around to collect, Jack locked him up in a pear tree and so sneaked out of the deal.

Eventually blacksmith Jack died. Heaven didn't want him. But when he went to hell, the devil threw him out. Jack was eating a turnip at the time. Quickly he picked up a burning coal and put it in the turnip to make a lantern. This Jack, too, had to walk the earth until Judgment Day.

56

The radish is one of the oldest vegetables in the world. Nobody knows quite where it started out. No wild forms have been found. However, most researchers think the radish began its history in China. The oldest written record of the radish comes from China in 1100 B.C.

Egyptian pharaohs thought the radish was just wonderful. They pressed needed oil out of its seeds. There were radish pictures painted on the walls of their pyramid tombs. The ancient Greeks also prized radishes. They placed radishes on gold plates and presented them in temples to one of their gods, Apollo. The word *radish* comes from the Latin word *radix*, or root.

Radish
Raphanus sativus

The ancient Romans had another use for radishes. They threw them at unpopular political speakers.

In medieval Europe, the spicy radish had many uses, including magic and medicine. If a person appeared mentally ill, eating radishes was supposed to be a cure. Radishes were also used to treat rheumatism, headaches, snake bite, baldness, and warts. One doctor wrote, "The radice quickeneth the wittes of the senses. It also taketh away blacke and blewe markes."

Dutch ships brought radish seeds to England in the sixteenth century. Soon the English ate radishes before meals to create a hearty appetite. The American colonists also put radishes in their gardens. Radishes are quite easy to grow. From seed to eating size takes only 30 days. An early American breakfast might have been something like bread, butter, brown sugar, and radishes—all washed down with tea.

You see red radishes most often in the market. But there are white, purplish, scarlet, and black radishes, too.

Spinach probably started its travels in ancient Persia, now Iran. Its name there was *isfanakh*, meaning "green hand." This sounds something like spinach, and is the base of our modern word. The Persians first grew *isfanakh* as greenery for their prized long-haired cats to chew on. As the years passed, spinach was used as a medicine for humans as well as a food.

By 150 B.C., spinach was growing in China. Large areas of green spinach grew around the many Chinese rice fields, or paddies.

In about A.D. 1000, Moorish travelers brought spinach seeds to Spain. The Spanish word is *espinaca*. The Crusaders also carried seed through Europe. By A.D. 1500, spinach was growing in England.

Spinach

Spinacia oleracea

No one is certain who brought "spynadg" to North America, but by the 1600s, it was listed among garden seeds for spring planting in the American colonies.

Spinach is very high in vitamin A, and also contains vitamin C, calcium, iron, protein, phosphorus, and B vitamins. For a long time it wasn't a very popular vegetable. But then the newspapers started carrying a comic strip about Popeye the Sailor Man.

Your parents might remember this comic strip. Popeye was a skinny man with big muscles who could get rid of bullies with a single punch. Those muscles supposedly came from eating a lot of spinach. That made spinach quite popular. Now we know that muscles come from exercise. But many people still eat spinach and like it.

One early English cook wrote that making hot breakfast cereal, or porridge, with a mixture of spinach and oatmeal seemed like a very good idea.

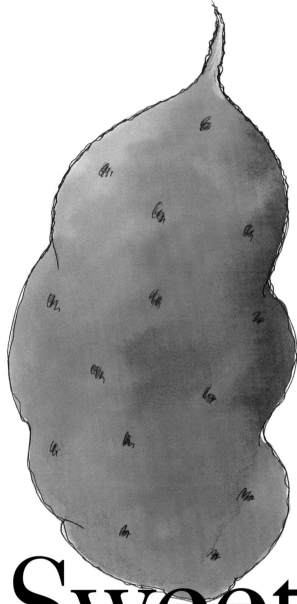

sweet potatoes may have originated in Peru. This potato is really the thickened root of a trailing tropical vine similar to our morning glory. The local tribes, finding the vine had wide edible roots, took to growing it in their garden. Through selective planting, eventually the roots became as large as potatoes. These roots had the Indian name *batatas*. The sweet potato became a basic food in Central and South America, Mexico, and the West Indies.

It is possible that Peruvian sailors, driven off course by the wind, brought plants to tropical areas of the New World. Christopher Columbus wrote that several types of sweet potatoes were served as food after his ships docked in St. Thomas. He also wrote about sweet potato bread, or *aje* bread.

Sweet Potato
Ipomea batatas

Columbus carried sweet potatoes to Spain. From there they were brought to Portugal, then to England, where at first they were called *Spanish potatoes*.

Sweet potatoes were also called potatoes. Because of this word mix-up, it is very difficult to trace the history of the sweet potato. It wasn't until 1775 that the sweet potato was actually given its own name in the dictionary.

Sweet potatoes have a lot of vitamin A, plus vitamins C and B, potassium, calcium, and phosphorus. Not many people confuse a sweet potato with a white potato today. But sweet potatoes are often confused with yams, a native of West Africa. True yams are very seldom seen in the supermarket. But you will see sweet potatoes with moist, deep orange insides that are called *yams*.

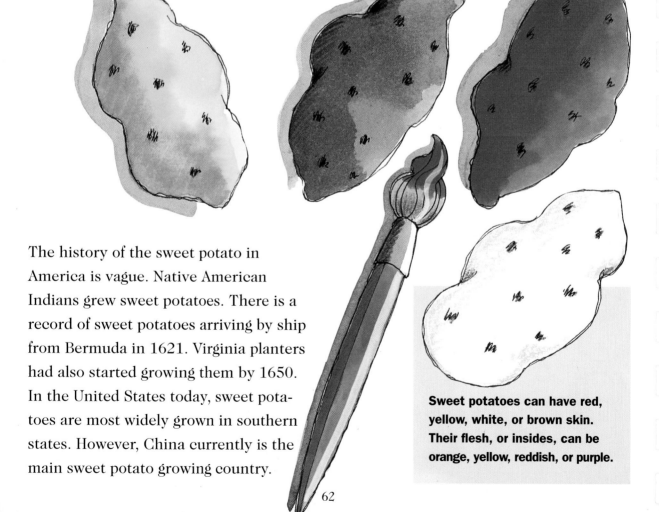

The history of the sweet potato in America is vague. Native American Indians grew sweet potatoes. There is a record of sweet potatoes arriving by ship from Bermuda in 1621. Virginia planters had also started growing them by 1650. In the United States today, sweet potatoes are most widely grown in southern states. However, China currently is the main sweet potato growing country.

Sweet potatoes can have red, yellow, white, or brown skin. Their flesh, or insides, can be orange, yellow, reddish, or purple.

Tomatl, or tomatoes, probably started out in the Andes Mountains of Peru. Small wild tomatoes still grow there today.

When Spanish explorers, led by Hernando Cortes, met the ruling Aztec of Mexico in about 1519, they also saw the pretty yellow-flowered "tomatl" vines for the first time. Tomato seeds along with Aztec gold were carried as cargo back to Spain.

Tomato
Lycopersicon esculentum

Tomatoes are quite easy to grow if there's sun and a lot of water. Soon *tomate* vines were quite popular in Spanish gardens. Their popularity increased because eating a tomato was supposed to make a person more romantic. Some healers of the time thought the shape of a tomato resembled the shape of a human heart. Does it?

A Moorish visitor to Seville, Spain, carried seeds to Morocco. Soon tomatoes were growing there. An Italian sailor went ashore at Tangier, Morocco. He took some tomatoes home to Italy.

There are yellow, red, pink, orange, and green tomatoes. One of the tomatoes to reach Italy was yellow. At first the Italians called it *pomo dei Mori*, or "Moors' apple." That became *pomi d'oro*, or "apple of gold." But the heart-shaped idea won out. The next Italian name was *poma amoris*, or "the apple of love."

The tomato became *pomme d'amour*, or love apple, in French. But with all the names, the pretty vine was still used mostly as a garden decoration rather than food. In many places, people believed the yellowish fruits were somewhat poisonous. A nickname was *wolf peach*, referring to bait used to poison wolves.

By the 1770s, tomatoes, or "the love apple," had arrived in America. But not to applause. Early American settlers probably wouldn't have grown tomatoes at all, but those yellow flowers and the pretty green leaves looked so nice in the garden. However, settler children were told to stay away from the plant. The tomato itself, settlers had heard, was poisonous.

It wasn't until 1812 that Americans began doing a tomato turnabout. By then, the French had started using tomatoes in their famous gourmet foods. They still called it *pomme d'amour*.

When the French military occupied New Orleans, they used the "love apple" as part of their daily meals. From here the tomato slowly gained acceptance. Within 25 years, what was once thought of as a poison now became a "cure" for stomach problems of all kinds. It was also supposed to prevent the dreaded cholera, a highly contagious disease from which many settlers died.

The Pilgrims considered eating a tomato a sin equal to playing cards and dancing.

The University of California at Davis is home to a U.S. tomato genetic center. It has 2,600 different tomato types on record.

Today, if you have a vegetable garden, chances are you grow at least one tomato plant. You can grow them on patios and even sunny open windowsills. Try it! There are quarter-size tomatoes, such as Tiny Tim, and huge beefsteak tomatoes weighing over a pound. There's even a beefsteak tomato called *Abraham Lincoln*, and a white tomato called *Snow White*.

What's the hugest tomato? The world record is 7 pounds, 12 ounces (3.2 kilograms, 340 grams), and this top tomato was grown in Oklahoma. The grower says he talked nicely to his tomato plants. He also played country music for them. Can you do a plant experiment to find out whether playing music to a plant helps? You might try different types of music and even singing.

Tomatoes are the state fruit of Ohio. They contain vitamins A, C, and B, potassium, phosphorus, and calcium. Even if you haven't had a tomato today, maybe you have had some ketchup on a hamburger or hot dog. Today's ketchup, or catsup, began as *ketchap*. This was a spicy Malayan fish sauce made with various ingredients, including oysters, walnuts, shrimp, and, of course, tomatoes.

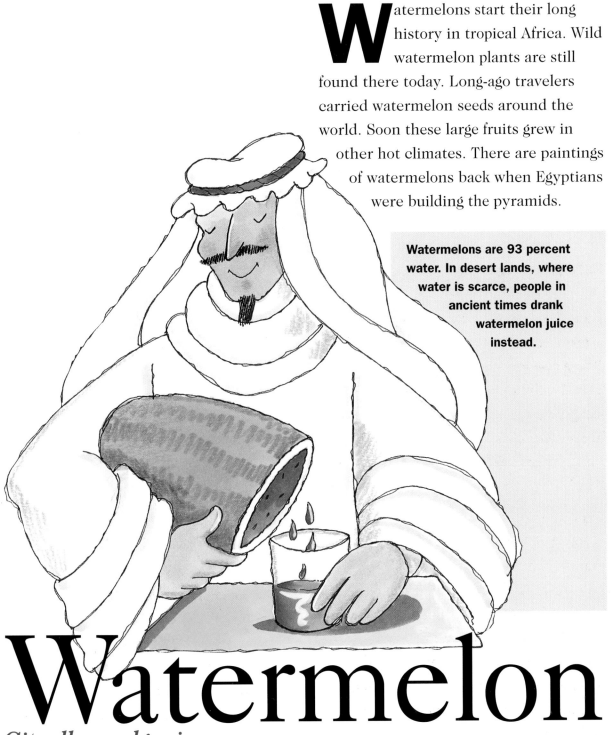

Watermelons start their long history in tropical Africa. Wild watermelon plants are still found there today. Long-ago travelers carried watermelon seeds around the world. Soon these large fruits grew in other hot climates. There are paintings of watermelons back when Egyptians were building the pyramids.

Watermelons are 93 percent water. In desert lands, where water is scarce, people in ancient times drank watermelon juice instead.

Watermelon
Citrullus vulgaris

Now taken for granted as summer eating in the United States, watermelons didn't get here until early colonists carried over some seeds. The first melons were small compared to modern types. They were eaten plain, used in cooking, and crushed for juice. Sometimes watermelon juice was used as a special drink given to sick people, hoping it would help cure them.

Many Native American Indian tribes adopted the watermelon as part of their regular crop. They called them *horse pumpkins*, claiming they smelled like a sweating horse. Among the Pueblo Indians, watermelons were given as gifts. Mojave, Cocopas, Maricopas, and Yuma Indians ate watermelon seeds. When crushed, watermelon seeds give off some oil. This was used as a cooking oil on Indian bread baking stones.

Watermelon seeds are still eaten in many parts of the world today. In Asia, the seeds are roasted and enjoyed like pumpkin seeds.

Today's watermelons have pulp that can be white, yellow, pale orange, red, and pink. How can you tell if a watermelon is ripe? Thump it. You may have to thump several to hear the difference in sounds. Perhaps you can try this in the classroom. The supermarket might not like all the booms, but your teacher can ask the manager if it would be all right on a class field trip.

A perfect watermelon for eating has a somewhat muffled sound when thumped. If you thump your chest, you hear that type of sound. An overripe melon has a heavier sound when thumped. What does it sound like when you thump on your stomach? It sounds like a very muffled drum. An underripe watermelon makes a clear sharp sound when thumped—like thumping lightly on your forehead.

Watermelon is related to the cucumber, pumpkin, and squash.

Watermelons grow best in warm regions, as in the southern United States. However, they will grow in Canada, too, if planted during summer heat. The smallest watermelons today are about 5 pounds (2.3 kilograms). The largest are over 100 pounds (45.4 kilograms).

Fun with Kitchen Fruits and Vegetables

Indoor Plant-Growing Basics

Before you begin working on any of the projects that follow, you should learn some basic information about growing plants indoors.

You must crush garden earth until it has no lumps. You can do this by putting it in a paper bag, then a plastic bag, and then stomping on it.

If you use garden earth, you may find weeds growing, too. When you are certain which is weed and which is your plant, take the weeds out.

If you want to make certain your garden earth has no weed seeds or insect eggs, you can bake it. But it smells when you do this. (Just so you know.) Use disposable pie pans or other disposable aluminum containers. Put a thin layer of earth in each pan. Have an adult set the oven to 180°F (82°C). Put containers in the oven for 30 minutes. Cool in a safe place. Do not touch them until they are cool.

2

If you can't get garden earth, perhaps an adult will buy you some potting soil at the store. This may make growing your plants easier.

Always place your container on a plate or pie tin so water does not get onto the furniture.

Never place a plant anywhere near a microwave oven or regular oven. The plant will bake from the hot air.

Never let a plant or plant seed dry out in the container. The young roots will die quickly, and even if you add water later, the plant may not recover.

Containers you can use are: jam and jelly jars, peanut butter jars, empty clean milk containers cut in half, coffee cans, very clean bleach containers with the top cut off, and cottage cheese containers. Clean containers by washing with soap and water and rinsing with water.

Don't waste the fruit because you want to use the seeds. You can eat the orange, avocado, mango, pomegranate, pineapple, or any other fruit here, as long as your hands are clean. Most fruits, such as apples, should be washed first.

What you need

1 seeds from 3 large ripe (soft) avocados
If your market has more than one avocado type, such as rough skinned and smooth, or different colors, try seeds from each. You can do this project with only 1 or 2 seeds, but 3 give you a better chance to get a plant. Some avocado types are easier to grow than others.

2 3 clean jars
You will need 1 jar for each seed. Jelly or jam jars are a good size.

3 about 20 toothpicks

4 water

Avocado

What to do

Wash the pit with warm water. Remove as much brown skin as you can with a kitchen brush. Any skin you leave on may develop a mold. But you can gently take this off later.

Poke 3 toothpicks, like a belt, into each avocado seed's middle. You have extra toothpicks, so if one breaks, use another. Some avocado seeds may have already started to split. Handle them carefully so they don't break open completely. If they do, throw away the parts and start again.

Put one seed into each jar. The toothpicks should hold the seed in place so it does not drop into the jar. The pointed end of the avocado seed must be up. The round end must be down. With some seeds, it may be hard to tell which end is round and which end is pointed. If so, look for a part that seems to have a little fold or tuck. That's the "round," or bottom, side.

Fill each jar with lukewarm water that covers the seed a little less than halfway. Place the jars in the shade. You can put them in a cabinet. The jars should never get cold. Change water once a week. Keep the water level a little below the middle of the avocado seed.

What will happen?

In one to three weeks the seed begins to split in half. At about that time, you will see white roots coming from the avocado bottom. It may take longer than this—even three months. Be patient. Some avocado seeds take longer to get started than others. This is true in nature, too. Soon after the roots come out, a green shoot will start growing from each avocado top.

When roots are 3 inches (7.6 centimeters) long, it is time to move the avocado to a container. It can be a ½-gallon (1.9-liter) milk carton, a larger jar, or a flowerpot. Put earth in the container. With a teaspoon, make a hole for the growing seed that is deep enough to hold the roots without bending them. Handle the seed gently, otherwise it may fall apart. Put it carefully in place. Put soil around the seed until it is half covered. Put the container on top of an old dish, so water doesn't leak out onto the furniture.

Give your plant some water, just until the earth feels damp. Place the container in a warm sunny place. Water just to keep soil damp. Too much water hurts the plant.

Soon you will have a nice green plant. As it gets bigger, you can put it in larger containers. Avocado plants won't grow fruit indoors. If you grow a few plants, you can try planting one outdoors in a sunny place. But remember to water it so that the earth stays damp.

What you need

1. 3 fresh beets with some green growth at top

2. 3 short glass jars or 3 leakproof cups or the bottom half of a one quart (1 liter) milk container

3. pebbles or small rocks

4. water

5. old pie pans to place under containers

What to do

Put 1 whole beet in each container, or 3 in the larger container. Surround beet bottoms with pebbles to hold them upright. Do not cover the beet more than halfway. Cover the beet bottom one-third of the way with water. Always keep water to that level.

What will happen?

Within a week, dark green leaves begin growing. They will grow for two weeks, then seem to die. Wait a bit. You may see a flower stalk with lavender flowers. The flowers will fade in a few days. Then you can throw out the plant.

Beet

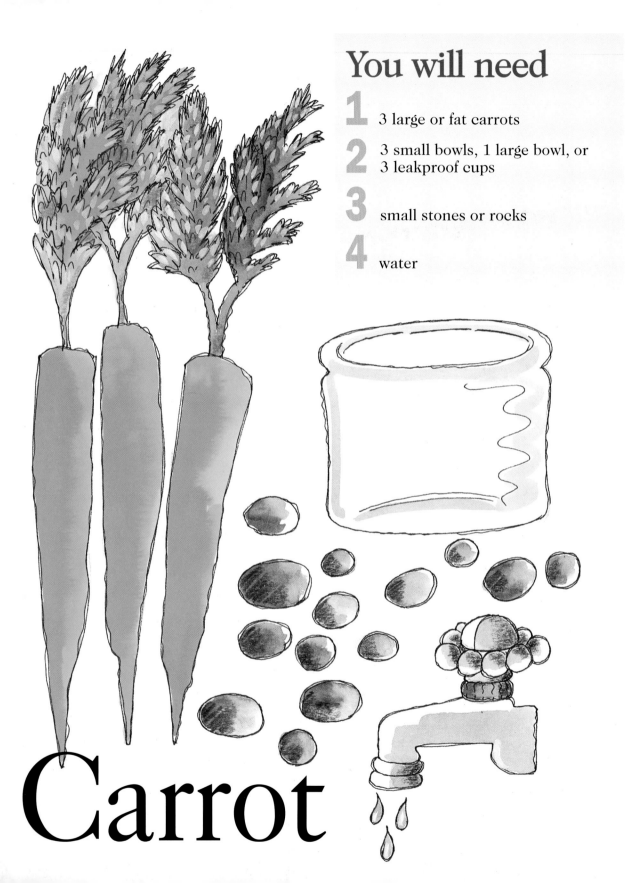

You will need

1 3 large or fat carrots

2 3 small bowls, 1 large bowl, or 3 leakproof cups

3 small stones or rocks

4 water

Carrot

What to do

Have an adult cut off 2 inches (5 centimeters) from each carrot top. Remove any old leaves. Place the top, cut side down, in the container. Add water until the carrots are halfway covered. Place rocks around the carrot to hold it in place. If you have 3 carrots in one container, such as a large leakproof cup, they will hold each other up. Now put the bowl in a bright place, but not too sunny or too hot.

What will happen?

In a week, little green leaves will start growing from the carrot top. Now place your container in a sunny place. Make certain the container always has water in it. You will soon have feathery green leaves. Each carrot top only has enough food for the leaves for about three weeks. Then that plant will die. But you can always put in more carrot tops.

What you need

1 3 pieces of fresh gingerroot

2 a 6-inch (15-centimeter) wide bowl or pot, or a ½-gallon (1.9-liter) clean, empty milk container cut in half for each piece of gingerroot

3 earth without lumps

4 water

Gingerroot

What to do

Fill each container two-thirds full with earth. Place gingerroot on top. Cover gingerroot about $1/2$ inch (1.3 centimeters) with earth. Water until damp. Put pots in a well-lit area, but not too sunny. Keep damp.

What will happen?

In about a month, you will see little beige bumps at the end of some gingerroot *rhizome* "fingers." (Note: *rhizome* is the scientific word for "rootlike stem.") In a while, these bumps will become stems or *stalks*. They will grow for two months, maybe more. Always keep the earth damp.

You can try moving, or *transplanting*, your ginger plants outside after a few months if the weather is nice and cold weather is not expected. Ginger needs warmth and plenty of water.

What you need

1 seeds from a lemon, orange, and/or grapefruit
Try 3 seeds of each. Pick the biggest ones. Be sure to mark each container so you don't forget which is which.

2 clean empty milk cartons, jars, or cans

3 earth without lumps

4 a pie pan to place under the container

5 water

6 sandwich bag

7 waxed paper

Lemon, Orange, and Grapefruit

What to do

Soak seeds overnight in a dish. Have an adult cut the milk cartons in half. Use the bottom half as your plant container. Put the cartons on a plate or empty pie pan so water does not leak through.

Fill the container a little more than halfway with earth. Poke seeds into the earth about ¹/₂ inch (1.3 centimeters) down. Put 1 or 2 seeds in each container. Cover the container top with waxed paper. Hold this in place loosely with a rubber band. You can cover a small container with a sandwich bag. Place the container in a warm, not hot, place. Keep the earth damp.

What will happen?

In about three weeks, you will see small plants with green shiny leaves. Take the cover off the container. Place it in a very sunny place. Water once a week, just so the earth is damp.

If your plant grows too big for its container, move it carefully to a bigger one. If the plant ever gets big enough, you might see flowers. But that takes a few years.

What you need

1 1 mango

2 a scrub brush

3 a large nail clipper or garden clipper

4 a scissors

5 earth without lumps

6 a clean empty peanut butter jar or a quart (1 liter) milk container cut in half

7 a pie pan to place under the container

8 water

Mango

What to do

Remove the seed from inside the mango. The seed is surrounded by a thick cardboardlike covering or *husk*. This husk has many soft hairlike fibers on it. Scrub the husk with a kitchen brush to remove as much orange fruit as possible. Let the husk dry overnight.

Have an adult clip off the tip ends of the husk. Don't cut too far in or you will damage the large seed inside. Using a scissors, an adult should carefully cut the husk open like an envelope. There is a big beige seed inside. It looks like a very large, flat lima bean.

Take this seed out and soak it overnight. Plant it lying flat in soil mix. Cover the seed with ½ inch (1.3 centimeters) of earth. Place the container in a warm sunny place where there is no wind or drafts. Keep the soil damp, not wet.

What will happen?

You will see shiny red leaves in three weeks. As the tree grows over many months, you may need to place it in a larger container. Not all mango seeds will sprout, so you may want to start with several.

What you need

1 3 big onions
You may want to try 3 different kinds of onions. Some onions are easier to grow than others.

2 3 jars or drinking glasses big enough to hold each onion without it rolling over

3 water

Onion

What to do

Put an onion in each jar, rounded side down. Put a little water in the jar, just enough to wet the onion bottom. Don't use too much water, or the onion will rot. Put the jar in a bright place.

What will happen?

Within a week, you will see white roots coming from the onion bulb bottom. In a few weeks, you will see long green leaves coming from the onion top. Food for the leaves comes from the bulb. Always keep the water covering the bulb bottom.

As your leaves grow, an adult may ask to snip off the tops to use for cooking. That is up to you. When your onion leaves are 4 inches (10 centimeters) high, you may want to have an adult cut open an onion. You can see how the leaves have started from the bulb center.

When the onion starts to get smaller and softer, its food supply is getting used up by the leaves. After a while, you will want to throw it out.

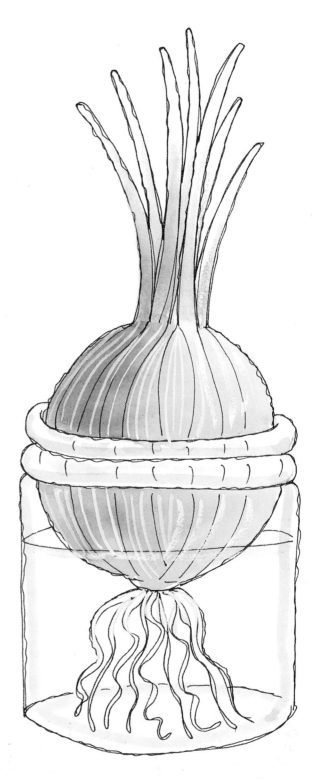

What you need

1 5 peach pits

2 peat moss

3 a plastic bag

4 earth without lumps

5 5 clean milk containers

6 water

Peach

What to do

Put the peach pits in the plastic bag. Put 2 cups (500 milliliters) peat moss in the bag. You can buy peat moss at most garden stores. Add ½ cup (125 milliliters) water. Close the bag tightly. Place in the refrigerator, not the freezer, for two months.

Why? Peach pits normally fall to the earth and lie there during the winter. They need that cold weather. In the spring, they will start growing.

Fill containers one-third full of peat moss and one-third full of earth. Take the seeds from the refrigerator and place one in each container. Set the containers in a warm shady place. Keep the earth damp. In three weeks, place the containers on a sunny window sill.

What will happen?

In a few weeks, you may see a small plant. Peach pits aren't always easy to grow. That's why you start with 5.

You can try the same method with cherry pits and apple seeds. Start with 10 seeds or pits of each. While you are waiting for them to grow, read about Johnny Appleseed.

What you need

1 5 fresh raw or unroasted peanuts
These are sold at seed stores, some health food stores, or in some supermarkets. You can also obtain them from seed catalogs. Roasted peanuts will not grow.

2 a container at least 6 inches (15 centimeters) wide and about 4 inches (10 centimeters) deep
If you can find a see-through gallon glass or plastic jar, that is better. Or you can use an old fish tank or plastic washtub. Place the container on something waterproof in case it leaks.

3 earth without lumps

4 water

Peanut

What to do

Remove shells from peanuts. Fill container about two-thirds full with earth. You can mix some sand with the earth to make it looser. Peanuts like sandy earth.

Place the peanuts on top of the earth. If you have a see-through container, place them near the outside so you can watch their growth better. Cover peanuts with 1 inch (2.5 centimeters) of earth. Water until the soil is damp. Keep in a warm sunny place, and keep damp, not wet.

What will happen

Wait two weeks. You should see round leaves. Wait until the tallest plant is 5 inches (12.7 centimeters) high. Gently remove the other plants and throw them away. (They may not grow if you plant them elsewhere.). There is not enough growing room for all the plants unless you have put them in a large fish tank.

Each plant will grow about a foot (30 centimeters) tall. It will have yellow flowers. When the flower petals fall off, much smaller flowers form on each stalk. The seed containers or fruits that develop from these small flowers will start bending toward the earth. They will push into the earth. At each tip, a peanut begins forming. Dig up the peanuts when the leaves begin to yellow.

What you need

1   1 fresh pineapple

2   a clean cottage cheese container
or large peanut butter jar

3   water

4   earth without lumps

Pineapple

What to do

Have an adult cut off the leafy top of the pineapple where it joins the fruit. The leaves are prickly, so be careful. Remove every bit of fruit. If you leave any, it will grow moldy.

Peel off the short bottom leaves so you have a 2-inch (5-centimeter) stem. Dry the pineapple top for two days. If it doesn't dry, it may rot before it roots.

Fill your container two-thirds full with earth. Place the pineapple top in the earth, cut side down. The soil should just come up to the leaf bottoms. Make certain the soil stays damp. Put the container in a shady place.

What will happen?

In about two weeks, you will see green leaves growing from the pineapple center. Move the container to a sunny place. The earth must stay damp. You can keep this plant for a long time.

Will you get a pineapple? Once in a while it does happen, but not very often.

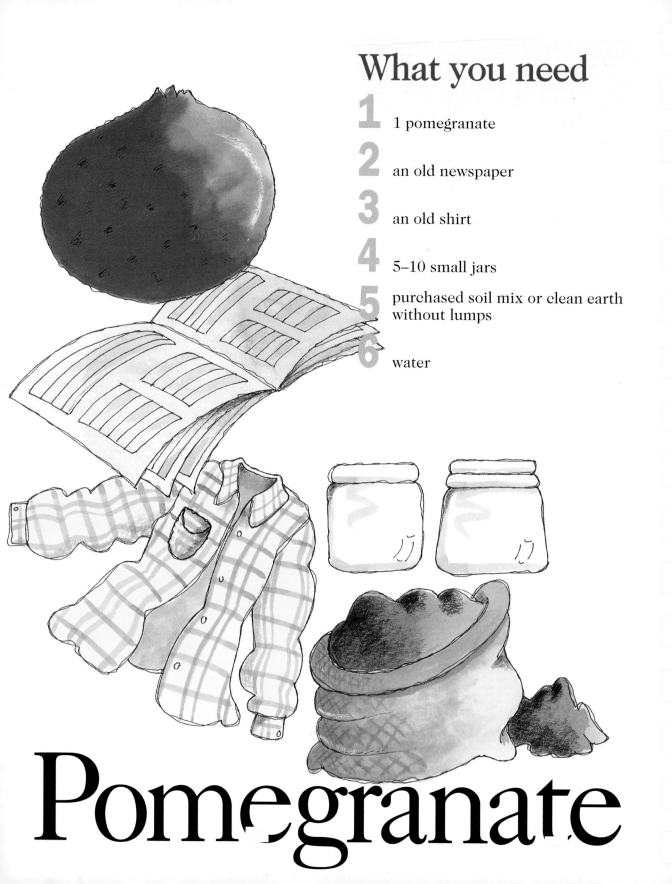

What you need

1   1 pomegranate

2   an old newspaper

3   an old shirt

4   5–10 small jars

5   purchased soil mix or clean earth without lumps

6   water

Pomegranate

What to do

Have an adult cut the pomegranate in half. Take out about 10 seeds. Place them on the newspaper. Put on your old shirt. Scrub the seeds with the newspaper to remove any fruit on top.

Fill the jars with earth. Place 1 or 2 seeds on the earth and cover with ½ inch (1.3 centimeters) of soil. Put a sandwich bag over the container tops. Place the containers in a warm bright place. Keep the earth damp.

What will happen?

In five to seven weeks you will see leaves coming out. At that time you can take off the bag. Be sure to keep the earth damp, not wet, at all times. If you take very good care of your plants, they may grow quite large. You will have to move them to bigger containers as they grow. After many years, fruit is possible.

What you need

1 2 small baking potatoes
Try to get those with tiny sprouting white buds on them. Many potatoes in supermarkets have been treated so they don't sprout. These will not grow into plants. You may want to try several different types of cooking potatoes to see what happens with each.

2 2 buckets at least 6 inches wide (15 centimeters) and 18 inches (45.7 centimeters) deep

3 purchased soil mix or earth without lumps

4 water

Potato

What to do

Fill the containers halfway with earth. Lay the potatoes on the earth. Cover them with 1 inch (2.5 centimeters) of earth. Water until slightly damp. Do not overwater. Place in a sunny, warm place.

In a week or so you will see leaves. After several weeks, you may see purple flowers, too. If your container is large enough, you may get little potatoes underground. Water to keep the earth slightly damp. If the earth is too wet, the potatoes will rot.

What to do

You can also try growing a baking potato in water. Put it in a clean jam or peanut butter jar so only the bottom stays wet. If you need toothpicks to hold it up, use them. You will see roots from the potato bottom and stems and leaves growing from the top.

Change the water once a week. If the plant doesn't start growing in two weeks, that potato may have been treated so it will not sprout. Try another one, or two.

What to do

Use potatoes that have little white sprouts all over. Have an adult cut them into pieces that each have 3 sprouts. Let these pieces dry overnight. Fill an empty clean ½-gallon (1.9-liter) milk container with earth. Place this container in an old pie pan so the water does not leak.

Put the potato pieces with sprouts about 3 inches (7.6 centimeters) down into the earth. Put the cut side down and the sprouts up. Water until damp. You may get a potato plant, just as a farmer does. Farmers plant their potatoes this way.

What you need

1 3 fresh radishes

2 3 small-size clean tomato sauce cans or leakproof cups, or a deep bowl

3 earth without lumps

4 water

Radish

What to do

Fill the containers halfway with earth. Place a radish in each container, pointed side down. If you have a larger container, you can place 2 or 3 radishes together. It's prettier. Water until the earth is damp. Place the containers in bright light. Add water as needed.

What will happen?

Within ten days you will see crinkled green leaves growing from the radish tops. You may even get a flower. The leaves use food from the radish. After a month, the food is all gone and the radish is smaller. Start new ones.

What you need

1 3 sweet potatoes
Sweet potatoes should be very easy to grow. But many sold in supermarkets have been specially treated not to sprout. Try to find those with little purple bumps on the skin, or a few skinny white roots sticking out. Using 3 sweet potatoes gives you a better chance of success.

2 3 glass or plastic jars
Large jam jars or medium-size peanut butter jars are the right size.

3 20 toothpicks

4 water

Sweet Potato

What to do

Find the pointed or narrower end of each sweet potato. Sometimes this end has a little "tail." This is the end that goes into the water.

Put 1 sweet potato in each jar. It should not touch the jar bottom. To hold it up, put 3 or 4 toothpicks around the middle, like a belt. Put water in the jar until it comes halfway up the sweet potato.

Place the jar in a warm, shady place in your room or in the kitchen. Make certain the water stays at the halfway mark. Change the water once a week. Use warmish water, never cold. If the potato water ever starts to smell, despite changing it weekly, that sweet potato may have been treated not to grow. Instead, it is spoiling. Throw it out and start again.

What will happen?

Within two weeks, you should see white roots from the bottom of a growing sweet potato. About two to three weeks later, you should see stems. Move the plant to a bright window.

Soon many ivylike leaves will grow. These become very pretty long stems or vines that will grow for two months or more. Keep adding water to the halfway mark so the roots don't dry out.

When your vines get long, you can use them to start new vines. Cut off 1 to 5 pieces of vine. Each should be about 6 inches (15 centimeters) long. Place these in a jam-size jar or mayonnaise-size jar filled with water. In a few days you will see roots. Then you will have more vines.

Add fresh water as the water evaporates. If you decorate the jars, you have nice presents for your family.

Indoor Plant-Growing Experiments with Food Seeds

Introduction

These indoor plant-growing experiments are easy to do. No complicated equipment is needed. All supplies and ingredients can be found at most local supermarkets, home improvement centers, or plant stores. If you can't find everything near you, a list of places offering seed catalogs is at the end of this book. An adult can order from these catalogs. Payment is by check, money order, or credit card. Orders take a few weeks to arrive.

Some seed catalogs are free; others cost less than $3. The letter you write might look like this:

3

(Date here)

(Name of seed company here)

Dear Sir or Madame:

I would like a copy of your seed catalog. Please send it to:

(your name)
(your address)

If there is a charge for this catalog, please let me know.

Sincerely,
(Then put your signature on the bottom.)

Write very neatly, or type, so the order person can read it.

Make certain to include your full address with zip code when writing to ask for a catalog. If the catalog will go to a classroom, include the teacher's name as well as the school and its address.

Once you have all the supplies and ingredients for each experiment, you can start your plant research right away. It is fun and interesting to compare your opinions before and after you do these experiments. Perhaps you thought all apples had the same number of seeds. Do they? Or that it didn't make any difference how deep you planted a seed. It does, doesn't it?

You may want to create your own experiments, too. Write down each step you take. That way, if you have to correct anything or repeat the experiment, you remember exactly what you have done.

Once you have done a few experiments, you will see fruits and vegetables in a new way. They are not just something to eat. They are living things that need the right amounts of air, water, and food to grow properly—just like you do.

Does cold, cool, or warm air make a difference to seed starting?

What you need

1 9 sponges (you can cut a sponge in half to make 2)

2 watercress seeds

3 mustard seeds

4 radish seeds

5 water

6 9 old pie pans or plates

Your opinion before the test:

What to do

Put each sponge in a container. Sprinkle 3 sponges with about 10 watercress seeds. Sprinkle 3 different sponges with about 10 mustard seeds. Sprinkle the 3 remaining sponges with about 10 radish seeds. Try to make the seeds go into the sponge holes.

Add water to the containers. Water should come to the middle of the sponge. Place one set of watercress, mustard, and radish sponges and their containers in the warmest part of the room. Place another set of watercress, mustard, and radish sponges and their containers on a counter where it is not too warm. Place the third set of watercress, mustard, and radish sponges in the refrigerator.

Sponges dry out very quickly, particularly if they are in the sun. Poke your sponge every day to see if it is still wet. If it starts to dry out, add water right away. If a sponge dries out, even for a short time, this experiment won't work properly. Being dry even a short time may kill the seed or seedling.

Keep a chart of which seeds sprout first. Do they sprout sooner in a warm growing spot or a cool growing spot? Did they sprout in the cold refrigerator?

Something to think about:

In southern states, the weather starts to warm up in March. In northern states and Canada it may still be very cold outside in March. Seed packets tell you planting months for that type of seed in each climate. Why? Do you think seeds will sprout outside where there is snow?

Your opinion after the test:

103

Do all apples have the same number of seeds?

What you need

1. 3 yellow apples of the same size
2. 3 green apples of the same size
3. 3 red apples of the same size
4. a kitchen knife to cut the apples
5. 12 paper napkins or paper towels
6. paste
7. cardboard
8. 1 red crayon and 1 black crayon

Your opinion before the test:

What to do

Using a red crayon, number each napkin from 1 to 9. Have an adult cut the apples in half. Place both halves of each apple on a numbered napkin. Remove the seeds from each apple and place them on the same napkin with their apple. Count the seeds. Write the number on each napkin with black crayon.

Now make a chart:

1. Red apple—xx seeds
2. Red apple—xx seeds
3. Red apple—xx seeds
4. Yellow apple—xx seeds
5. Yellow apple—xx seeds
6. Yellow apple—xx seeds
7. Green apple—xx seeds
8. Green apple—xx seeds
9. Green apple—xx seeds

You can paste the seeds on the chart if you want. Use colored paper to match the color of each apple if you want it to look very pretty. Do all apples have the same number of seeds? Do all apples of the same color have the same number of seeds?

This experiment method may be used to test fruits other than apples. Compare seed numbers in 3 oranges. Are they the same?

You can try this experiment with pears, oranges, grapefruit, and seeded grapes. After you are through counting the seeds, you may want to eat the fruit. Make certain you handled the fruit with clean hands if you want to eat it afterward.

Something to think about:

If you did not count pomegranate seeds, can you guess, from the results of the above seed counting tests, whether all pomegranates have the same number of seeds?

Your opinion after the test:

_____

_____

_____

105

How does water get from carrot roots into stems?

What you need

1 2 medium-size carrots with fresh leaves

2 2 water glasses

3 red food coloring

4 water

Carrots are taproots. *Taproots* are big roots growing down into the earth. Smaller roots grow from their sides. All roots absorb water from the earth and carry it to stems.

Your opinion before the test:

_____

_____

_____

What to do

Fill 2 glasses almost full of water. Put 10 drops of red food coloring in each glass. Have an adult cut off the bottom tip of 2 carrots. Put these carrots in the colored water.

Set the glasses on a sunny windowsill or close to bright lamplight. Let them sit at least two hours. Have an adult cut the carrot in half. Then have the adult cut the halved sections lengthwise (not across). Can you see how the red color travels? You may have to look very carefully to find the red areas if your carrots are younger and thinner, because these young carrots have smaller tubes that carry water.

Make a chart of these results.

Something to think about:

During dry weather, plants placed outdoors sometimes suffer from lack of water. Young plants have more problems than older ones. Why?

Your opinion after the test:

_____

_____

_____

How does water get from a celery stalk into its leaflets?

What you need

1 red food coloring

2 3 water glasses

3 a bunch of fresh celery with leaflets

Your opinion before the test:

_____

_____

_____

What to do

Fill each glass halfway with water. Place 10 drops of red food coloring in each glass. Have an adult cut 3 long celery stalks from the bunch just before you are ready to do this experiment. Place 1 celery stalk in each glass.

Put the 3 glasses near a sunny window or near a bright light.

Make a chart. Use a separate chart section for each celery stalk.

After one hour, remove the celery stalk from the first container. (You can label it *A* for your chart.) Have an adult cut off a bottom piece. Can you see how the colored water entered the stalk? Draw a picture of this in each section of your chart.

Now have an adult cut the celery at 1-inch (2.5-centimeter) intervals. Stop when you cannot see any more red dots. How many inches from the bottom was this? Record it on your chart.

Wait three hours. Examine the celery in the second container (labeled *B*). How high up has the red color traveled? Record this on your chart. Has the red color reached all the leaflets?

At each inspection, scrape some of the outer skin off your celery stalks. Do this from top to bottom. What do you see? Draw a picture of each stalk on your chart. Use crayons or colored pencils if you can.

Leave the celery in the third container (labeled *C*) overnight. In the morning, has the color reached all the leaflets? Each celery stalk has very small strawlike drinking tubes from its bottom to its leaflets.

Separate one of the largest leaflets. Try to copy the leaf form and all the red veins on a sheet of white paper. Can you see how they reach every section of the leaflet?

Your opinion after the test:

109

Can radish plants be too crowded to grow well?

What you need

1 3 clean cottage cheese containers, labeled *A*, *B*, and *C*

2 earth without lumps or purchased soil mix

3 2 packages of radish seeds

4 water

Your opinion before the test:

_____

_____

_____

What to do

Fill each container two-thirds full with soil. In container *A*, sprinkle an entire package of radish seeds. Sprinkle just a very, very thin layer of soil on top.

In container *B*, sprinkle one-half a package of radish seeds. Cover with just a very, very thin layer of soil—about $1/8$ inch (3 millimeters).

For container *C*, use just 5 radish seeds. Place these seeds as evenly as possible over the soil. Cover very lightly with soil.

Sprinkle each container with $1/4$ cup (60 milliliters) of water. Do this lightly so you don't push the little radish seeds deeper into the earth.

Put the containers by a sunny window. Check the soil every two days to make sure it is still damp. Little seedlings dry quickly, and even if you water them later, they may not recover. If a container dries out, this counting experiment will not work correctly.

At the end of one, two, three, and four weeks, describe what is happening in each container.

You may want to remove all but 1 radish plant from each container. What happens now?

Your opinion after the test:

_____

_____

_____

111

Can seeds be planted too deep to grow?

What you need

1. 1 package of radish seeds
2. 6 fresh or dried pea seeds
3. 6 fresh or dried bean seeds
4. 10 clean containers, at least 4 inches (10 centimeters) deep, labeled
5. earth without lumps
6. water

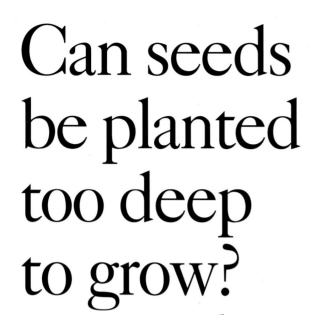

Your opinion before the test:

112

What to do

Soak dried pea or bean seeds overnight. Fill 3 containers with 1 inch (2.5 centimeters) of earth. Put 2 pea seeds in one container. Put 2 bean seeds in the second container. Sprinkle a few radish seeds in the third container. Cover all seeds with 3 inches (7.6 centimeters) of soil. Add ¼ cup (60 milliliters) of water to each container.

Fill 3 containers with 2 inches (5 centimeters) of earth. Put 2 pea seeds in the first container. Put 2 bean seeds in the second container. Sprinkle a few radish seeds in the third container. Cover all seeds with 2 inches (5 centimeters) of soil.

Fill 3 containers with 3 inches (7.6 centimeters) of earth. Put 2 pea seeds in the first container. Put 2 bean seeds in the second container. Sprinkle a few radish seeds in the third container. Cover all seeds with 1 inch (2.5 centimeters) of earth. Add ¼ cup (60 milliliters) of water to each container.

Fill 1 container with earth. Sprinkle a few radish seeds on top of the earth. Cover seeds with just a tiny bit of earth. Add ¼ cup (60 milliliters) of water to this container.

Place all the containers in a sunny, warm place. Do not let them dry out.

Keep a record of how the seeds grow. Which starts growing first? Second? Third? Wait three weeks. Are there any seeds that don't grow at all?

Something to think about:

If you do not try the experiment with tomato seeds, can you guess, from the above results, whether how deep you plant the seeds makes a difference to seedling growth?

Your opinion after the test:

_____

_____

_____

Do all lima bean seeds of the same size grow at the same rate?

Your opinion before the test:

_____

_____

_____

What you need

1 10 equal size lima beans

2 5 clear drinking glasses, labeled with different letters or numbers

3 about 10 white paper napkins or paper towels

4 water

5 a small ruler

6 a bowl

What to do

Soak 5 lima beans overnight in a bowl. Keep the rest of the beans in the package in case you want to repeat the experiment.

Wet the paper napkins and place them around the inside of each glass like a liner. Place 1 wet paper napkin in the center to keep everything in place.

Place 2 lima beans in each glass. Put the lima beans between the napkins and the glass so you can see them. The napkins will hold the beans in place. Pour about an inch (2.5 centimeters) of water into the container bottoms. Set the glasses in a warm, dark place, such as a kitchen cabinet. Wait a few days.

What will happen

Roots will appear first and then green leaves. As each lima bean sprouts, measure the sprout from top to bottom with your ruler. Write the measurements on a chart. Draw a picture of each sprout, too. Do this every day for a week. Make certain there is always water in the bottom of the glass. At the end of the week, mark down the final measurements.

Does each lima bean grow at the same rate?

You might want to repeat the experiment in a well-lit place. Scientists repeat experiments many times to make sure of results. Do a separate chart section for each time you repeat an experiment.

Since each type of seed is different, you cannot use the results from your lima bean experiment to predict how other seeds will grow under the same conditions. But you can do the experiment again with different types of seeds. Some seeds you might try are 10 corn, pea, lentil, or watermelon seeds.

Answer these questions:

1. Does each corn seed grow at the same rate?
2. Does each pea seed grow at the same rate?
3. Does each lentil seed grow at the same rate?

Something to think about:

If you did not test green pepper seeds, can you guess, from the results of the above growth experiments, whether they would all grow at the same rate?

Your opinion after the test:

Do bean seeds need moisture to start growing?

What you need

1 12 lima beans

2 12 kidney beans

3 12 pinto beans

4 4 glass containers

5 paper towels

6 water

If you can't find these beans at the market, you can try other types.

Your opinion before the test:

_____

_____

_____

What to do

Part 1: Soak 3 different type beans overnight: 1 lima, 1 kidney, and 1 pinto. Fill 1 glass with very wet paper towels. Put 1 soaked bean of each type around the edge of the container so that you can see the beans through the glass. The container will now have 3 beans in it. Mark *A*, *B*, or *C* where each bean type is. Make a note of this on your experiment sheet.

Part 2: Soak 3 different type beans overnight: 1 lima, 1 kidney, and 1 pinto. Fill 1 glass with dry paper towels. Put 1 soaked bean of each type around the edge of the glass. The glass will now have 3 beans in it. Mark *D*, *E*, or *F* to identify the beans. Make a note of this on your experiment sheet so you remember which bean is which.

Part 3: Use 3 different type beans that have not been soaked. Fill 1 glass with the very wet paper towels. Put 1 dry bean of each type around the edge of this container. The container will now hold 3 beans: 1 lima, 1 kidney, and 1 pinto. Mark the container *G*, *H*, or *I* where each bean type is. Make a note of this on your experiment sheet, so you remember which bean is which.

Part 4: Use 3 different type beans that have not been soaked. Fill 1 glass with dry paper towels. Put 1 dry bean of each type around the edge of this container so that you can see the beans through the glass. The container will now hold 3 beans: 1 lima, 1 kidney, and 1 pinto. Mark the container *J*, *K*, or *L* where each bean type is. Make a note of this on your experiment sheet.

Place the containers in a dark cabinet. Open the cabinet door and look at the containers each day. When you see any bean sprouting, write how many days it took on your chart. At the end of ten days, stop the experiment.

Your opinion after the test:

117

Do pea plants need light to start growing?

What you need

1 12 peas, either dried or fresh

2 4 clean glass or plastic containers, about 1-cup (250 milliliters) size

3 earth without lumps

4 4 sandwich bags

Your opinion before the test:

_____

_____

_____

118

What to do

Soak dried peas overnight. Fresh peas may be used directly from the pea pod. Fill containers two-thirds full with earth. Place 3 pea seeds in each container. Push about ½ inch (1.3 centimeters) down. Cover with earth. Add ¼ cup (60 milliliters) of water to each container. Cover each container with a sandwich bag. Mark the containers *A*, *B*, *C*, and *D*.

Place container *A* by a sunny window. Place container *B* by a bright lamp that remains on for at least six hours per day. Place container *C* on a countertop away from bright light. Place container *D* on a closed cabinet shelf.

Make a note on your chart when each pea seed starts growing. Then wait a week. Now place your pea plant containers next to each other. Compare their growth. Describe this on your chart. Draw pictures, too.

You may try this experiment method with other seeds, such as mustard seed and mung beans.

Something to think about:

If you do not try the experiment with grass seeds, can you guess, from the above results, whether light makes a difference to seedling growth?

An additional experiment:
Do pea plants need light to keep growing?

Put your pea plant containers back in their growing spaces: sunlight, bright light, medium light, and no light. Do not put the sandwich bags on them. Make certain the soil stays slightly damp. Wait another week. Mark your results on a chart. Then wait a third week. Mark your results on a chart.

Your opinion after the test:

_____

_____

_____

Your opinion after the test:

_____

_____

_____

Are all flowers either male or female?

What you need

1 5 different garden flowers

2 a tweezers

3 a magnifying glass

4 white paper

5 cellophane tape or white paste

Your opinion before the test:

What to do

In winter, flowers may be hard to find. But in spring and summer, you can choose from many. Weed flowers are fine for this project. If you can find a flower on a vegetable plant or fruit tree, that's even better. Have an adult cut each flower with at least a 3-inch (7.6-centimeter) long stem.

Place each flower on a separate sheet of white paper. Label the paper with the plant name if you know it. Take the largest flower apart first. Tape or paste the petals to the paper.

Tape or paste a piece of stem to the paper. Now look for the *stamens*. Stamens are skinny threadlike strands in the flower center. These are the male part of the flower.

On top of each male stamen is an *anther*. It has golden yellow pollen grains on it. Pollen is what bees collect for their hives. Use your tweezers to remove the pollen. Carefully tape some pollen grains to the paper.

If you don't find any stamens, make a note of this on your display paper. Go on to the next step.

In the flower center there is a round or slim ball. This is the *pistil*. It is the female part of the flower. Open it up. You will see many very tiny future seeds. These are called *ovules*. Tape the ovules to your display paper. If you don't find the pistil, make a note of this on your display paper.

Do this for each flower you have. Do all have both stamens and pistils?

When you touch the pollen, some comes off on your fingertips. If you touch the pistil afterward, look at it with your magnifying glass. Do you see some pollen grains on the pistil? When pollen grains reach the pistil of a growing flower, the ovules start becoming seeds of future plants.

Something to think about:

What purpose do you think bees, wasps, and other insects that go from flower to flower have in the garden? What happens if insecticides kill the bees?

Your opinion after the test:

_____

_____

_____

Do radish seedlings always grow toward light?

What you need

1. some radish seeds

2. a small glass jar with a cover

3. absorbent cotton

4. water

Your opinion before the test:

_____
_____
_____

What to do

Stuff the jar with cotton. Sprinkle radish seeds into the jar. Add enough water to dampen the cotton. Cover the container. Put the container right side up in a well-lit area. After four days, turn the jar upside down. Watch what happens to the leaves.

You can try this experiment with cress or other small seeds, too.

Something to think about:

If you planted pumpkins in a garden, and there was more sun in one direction than another, which way would you expect pumpkin seedlings to grow?

Your opinion after the test:

_____

_____

_____

Do roots hold soil in place?

What you need

1. 5 radish seeds

2. 5 mustard seeds

3. 2 glass or plastic containers, about 1-cup (250-milliliter) size

4. earth without lumps

5. water

Your opinion before the test:

_____

_____

_____

What to do

Fill both containers two-thirds full of earth. Place 5 radish seeds in 1 container. Place 5 mustard seeds in another container. Cover them very, very lightly with earth. Add ¼ cup (60 milliliters) of water to each container. Place in a sunny area or near a bright light. Make certain that the soil stays slightly damp.

At the end of two weeks, empty the radish container onto some newspaper. Empty the mustard seed container onto another newspaper. What shape does the earth have? Why?

Something to think about:

If a fire burns away plants from a hillside, what will happen to the soil when it rains heavily?

Your opinion after the test:

_____

_____

_____

Will bean plants grow in salted earth?

What you need

1   6 lima beans, either dried or fresh

2   6 kidney beans

3   6 pinto beans

4   9 clean glass or plastic containers, about 1-cup (250-milliliter) size

5   earth without lumps

6   salt

7   sandwich bags

8   water

Your opinion before the test:

_____

_____

_____

What to do

Soak dried beans overnight. Fill each container two-thirds full of earth. Place 2 bean seeds of the same type in each container. Push the bean seeds ½ inch (1.3 centimeters) down and cover with earth. Mark the containers with a letter so you can tell what is in each one. Record this on a chart.

Add ¼ cup (60 milliliters) of plain water to 1 lima bean, 1 kidney bean, and 1 pinto bean container. Make certain you label the containers and record which one is which on your chart.

Then add ¼ cup (60 milliliters) of water with 1 teaspoon of salt to a different lima bean, kidney bean, and pinto bean container. Label the containers and record them.

Now add ¼ cup (60 milliliters) of water with 1 tablespoon (15 milliliters) of salt to the remaining lima bean, kidney bean, and pinto bean containers. Label the containers and record them. Cover each container with a sandwich bag.

Place the containers where they will get at least six hours of bright light daily. At the end of one week, measure any growth. Record your measurements. Then describe the growth on your chart.

Your opinion after the test:

_____

_____

_____

Does all soil have the same ingredient mixture?

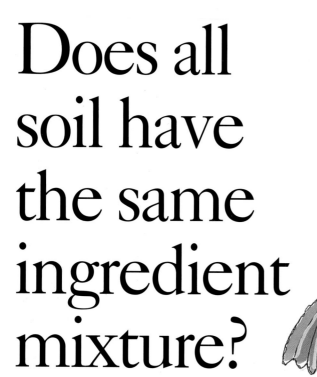

There are three basic soil ingredients: clay, silt, and sand.

What you need

1 a quart jar with a lid

2 earth from 3 different places, including purchased soil mix

3 crayons of various colors

4 water

Your opinion before the test:

_____

_____

_____

What to do

Fill the jar about two-thirds full of water. Add soil from one sample until the jar is almost full. Screw on the top. Shake the container well. Put the container on a flat counter. Wait one hour.

Sand goes to the bottom first. Silt settles down next. Clay particles are smaller and lighter, so they settle down last. You can see the layers in your jar. Draw a picture of this using different colored crayons. Label the picture.

Empty the jar outside. Wash it out. Now use soil from your second sample. You might have collected this soil from a different part of town, perhaps when you were visiting a relative. If the relative has a lovely garden, that's even better for this test. Repeat the test. Draw a picture of the results and label it.

Empty the jar outside. Wash it out. Then repeat the experiment again. But this time, use potting soil from the store. What happens? Draw a picture of the results. Label the picture.

Your opinion after the test:

_____

_____

_____

129

Do lima bean seeds need rich soil to start growing?

What you need

1 9 lima beans, fresh or dried

2 3 glass or plastic containers about 1-cup (250-milliliter) size

3 sand

4 garden earth

5 potting soil

6 water

Your opinion before the test:
_____
_____
_____

What to do

Fill each container two-thirds full of sand, earth, or potting soil. Label the containers A, B, and C. Make a record of what is in each container.

Put 3 lima beans, eye planted down, on the soil. Cover with ½ inch (1.3 centimeters) of the same material as in the container: sand, garden earth, or potting soil.

Give each container ¼ cup (60 milliliters) of water. Place near a sunny window or in a warm, well-lit place. Keep damp. At the end of one week, record what you see in each container.

Do lima beans need rich soil to keep growing?

Keep the 3 containers on the sunny windowsill or in a well-lit, warm area. Make a note of what happens at the two-week mark. Record your conclusion at the end of three weeks.

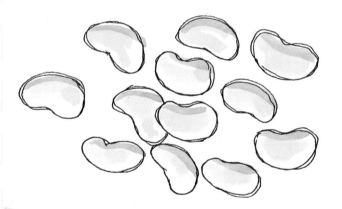

Do all vegetable leaves have the same vein pattern?

What you need

1 3 types of vegetable leaves (possibly: 3 each of beet, radish, spinach, celery, lettuce, pumpkin, or squash leaves)

2 white paper

3 a pencil

Your opinion before the test:

_____

_____

_____

What to do

Sit near a good light.
Copy each leaf shape onto a separate
piece of paper.
Copy each vein pattern onto its leaf
shape.

Something to think about:

Do you think it is possible to identify a
vegetable type by its leaf?

Your opinion
after the test:

_____
_____
_____

Can bean plants get too much water?

What you need

1 18 bean seeds, either dried or fresh

2 3 clean containers, about 1-cup (250-milliters) size

3 earth without lumps

4 water

5 ruler

6 sandwich bags

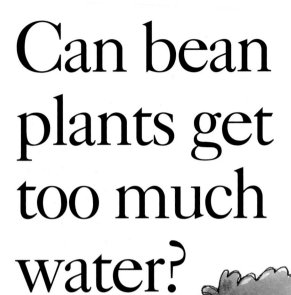

Your opinion before the test:

_____

_____

_____

134

What to do

Soak dried beans overnight. Do not soak fresh beans. Fill containers two-thirds full of earth. Place 3 bean seeds in each container. Push each about ½ inch (1.3 centimeters) down. Cover with earth. Mark each container with a letter: *A*, *B*, or *C*. Make a record of what you do with each container.

Put ¼ cup (60 milliliters) of water in container *A*. Put ⅓ cup (75 milliliters) of water in container *B*. Place ½ cup (125 milliliters) of water in container *C*. Put the 3 containers by a sunny window. Add the same amount of water as the original on day 3. Record the day you see any seedlings appear. On day 7, dig out all the seeds and put them on a sheet of white paper. What do the seeds look like? Record the results.

Now do the second part of this experiment:

Empty the containers you have used above. Fill each container two-thirds full of new dry earth. Place 3 bean seeds in each container. Push each about ½ inch (1.3 centimeters) down. Cover with earth. Mark each container *D*, *E*, or *F*. Add ¼ cup (60 milliliters) of water to each container. Cover each container with a sandwich bag. Place in a sunny, warm area. Wait one week.

Using a ruler, record any growth that you see. Now add ¼ cup (60 milliliters) of water to container *D*. Add ⅓ cup (75 milliliters) of water to container *E*. Add ½ cup (125 milliliters)of water to container *F*. Repeat this procedure in three days. At the end of a second week, measure growth and record your observations.

Something to think about:

Can you guess, from the above results, whether too much water for a particular type plant makes a difference to that plant's growth?

Information:

There are air spaces between soil particles. Roots take up this air. A plant needs air in order to grow. Water fills up air spaces.

Your opinion after the test:

135

Popcorn
taste tester:

Does all plain popcorn taste alike?

What you need

1. 5 different brands of unflavored popcorn
2. a microwave oven
3. 5 taste testers
4. sandwich bags or bowls
5. a score sheet
6. a microwave popcorn popper

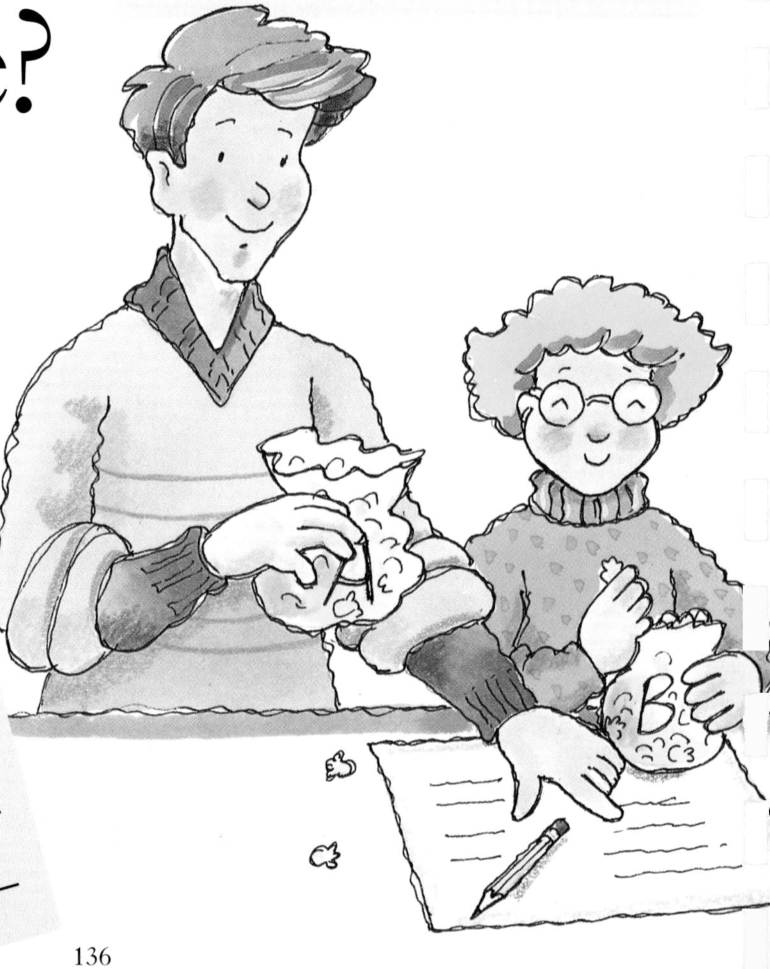

Your opinion before the test:

____

____

____

What to do

The adult will pop different types of popcorn in the microwave. Be sure to use at least one high-priced brand as well as the lowest-priced brand. Include microwavable popcorn and regular popcorn. Do not use flavored popcorn, as it changes the test results. The adult will divide the popcorn after popping. Each tester will get one sandwich bag of each kind. The sandwich bags will be labeled *A*, *B*, *C*, *D*, and *E*. No one will know what is in each bag except the adult or appointed scorekeeper.

Each taste tester will grade the popcorn on a taste test of 5 best to 0 worst. The scorekeeper will then place the results on a central chart. The popcorn getting the most 5 scores is the best tasting. The popcorn getting the most 4 scores is the second best tasting, and so on.

Something to think about:

Do you think this is a fair way to do a taste test? How would you improve it?

If you were to come up with an advertising slogan for the "best" popcorn, what would it be?

Your opinion after the test:

_____

_____

_____

Raising Earthworms, Pill Bugs, and Snails

Insects and other small crawling creatures are part of every outdoor garden. They provide food for birds and other animals, and also work to keep a garden healthy and clean.

In this book, you are gardening indoors. This gives you a chance to study a few small garden creatures up close. Watch how an earthworm moves through the earth. Study how the snail works as a garbage disposal. And maybe, if you're lucky, you'll see a mother pill bug carrying her babies around in a pouch.

4

Information

There are many different kinds of earthworms. In tropical rain forests, some live only in trees. Others live on the top of tall mountains, in the mud of deep lakes, or even on ocean shores.

Color and sizes vary. A Philippine earthworm is bright yellow with bluish spots. An Australian earthworm can stretch to 12 feet (3.7 meters), and looks like a snake. For this project, use the garden earthworm you find in earth around your apartment, house, or schoolyard. It is pale red and up to 4 inches (10 centimeters) long.

What you need

1 2 clean 1-gallon (3.8-liter) jars

2 2 covers (with holes) for the containers

3 earth without too many lumps

4 10 earthworms

5 an old dark-colored pillowcase

6 water

Earthworms

If the earth is very dry, earthworms may live too deep for you to find them easily. You can buy fishing worms, or "red wigglers," at bait shops.

An earthworm pushes through soft earth with the point of its head. Which end is the head? It is part with the swollen fleshy band near it.

If the earthworm can't push its way through hard ground, it eats its way through the earth. As the earthworm digests the organic food material in the earth, it breaks the earth up into very tiny pieces. This makes it easier for plant roots to use the earth as their food.

An earthworm tunnels down as deep as 8 feet (2.4 meters). These tunnels help bring air and water to plant roots. In good farmland, there can be as many as 2 million earthworms per acre. Of course, you don't see them. Earthworms must stay damp. The sun will quickly dry them out and kill them.

What to do

After you carefully dig the earthworms out, put them in a container filled with damp, loose earth. Cover this collection container with a lid. The lid must have airholes. Keep the container in a cool, not cold, place for a short time.

Now fill your second container about one-third full with earth. Scatter a torn-up lettuce leaf on top of this earth. Cover with about 1 cup of earth. Put in another torn-up lettuce leaf. Now fill the container with earth until it is almost full. Sprinkle about 1 cup of water into the container. Let it soak in. All the earth should be damp but not wet.

Now gently pour the earthworms into the second container. Put this container in a cool, very shady place. Light equals sun to an earthworm and makes it very uncomfortable. Cover the container. Make certain the cover has airholes. Whenever the soil just starts to feel dry to your fingertip, add a bit more water. Don't add too much water. Garden earthworms will drown in too much water.

From time to time, you can add a tablespoon of coffee grounds, a few teaspoons of oatmeal or cornmeal, a quarter piece of bread, or some fruit skins. Poke this food into the earth so it is all covered up. If you poke it near the jar glass, you can watch it disappear. Once a month add a piece of crushed eggshell.

141

When you are not watching your earthworms, keep an old pillowcase or cloth wrapped around the container to keep out the light. Do not cover the top, which has airholes.

If at any time the container smells rotten, you are keeping the container too wet. If your worms start to die, the container may be too wet, too dry, or too hot. Change the location.

If they are comfortable, your earthworms may mate. Earthworm eggs begin to grow under that swollen fleshy band near the head. When ready, the egg grouping, or *capsule*, slips out and moves along the worm's body to the front of its head. There it drops off. If you see a worm with a yellow ball on the tip of its head, it is becoming a parent.

Baby earthworms are white and thread-like. They become adults in three months. They can live up to four years. If this project is done at school, before summer vacation you should always dig a hole and place your worms back in the earth. Dampen it a bit so they are comfortable in their new home.

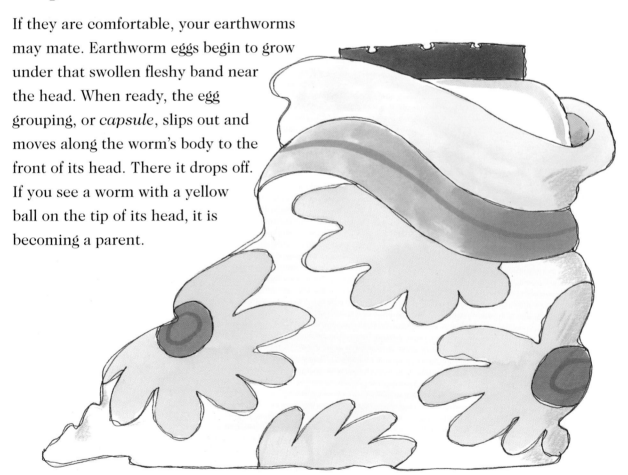

Earthworm projects

At the time you collect soil for your earthworm container, put some of the same soil in a separate plastic container. Don't do anything with this soil. After a month, compare your earthworm soil with the nonearthworm soil. What is the difference?

You can try filling a separate earthworm container with a mix of shredded newspaper and earth. Keep this damp, too. Will worms eat newspaper? If so, how long does it take for the newspaper to disappear?

After three months you will have earthworm compost. This is very good earth for growing plants. Try growing some of your kitchen seeds or herbs three different ways: in one-third earthworm compost and two-thirds regular earth, in all earthworm compost, and in all regular earth. Which grows the best? A hint: All earthworm compost is so rich it may be too much for plants.

Information

Pill bugs and sow bugs are not bugs or insects. They are related to lobsters, crabs and shrimp—all *crustaceans*. Long ago, pill bug ancestors crawled out of their ocean home onto land. But today's pill bugs still must always stay where it is cool and damp. You must never let your pill bugs or their home get warm or dried out.

What you need

1 a heavy plastic container at least 12 inches (30 centimeters) wide and 6 inches (15 centimeters) deep, or a 1-gallon (3.8-liter) jar

2 cardboard with holes in it

3 earth without lumps

4 paper towels

5 about 10 sow bugs or pill bugs

Sow Bugs/ Pill Bugs

Pick up a pill bug or sow bug very gently. Look at it closely. Which do you have? Pill bugs curl up in a ball when frightened. Sow bugs hump up in a bump. Sow bugs also have two tiny pointed tails. Pill bugs have no tail at all. Most people cannot tell the difference. But now you can. There are regional names for pill bugs and sow bugs, including bibble bug, wood louse, monkey pea, slater, and roly-poly.

When looking at your pill bug or sow bug, count its legs. There are seven pairs, or 14 legs. There are also two feelers, or *antennae*, at the front of its body. At the end of each feeler is an eye. These eyes see only light and dark. Do not keep your pill bug out of the container very long. Sun dries it out. Light hurts it.

What to do

Fill the plastic container or glass jar one-half full of loose earth. Place a double layer of paper towels over the earth. The paper towels must always be kept wet. Don't forget. If you have a large enough container, you can half bury a small empty can on its side in the earth. Pill bugs will like this special hiding cave.

Now have an adult collect your pill bugs or sow bugs. The best place to look is under any outdoor place that stays cool, dark, and damp in the daytime. The adult should wear gloves and use a stick to turn over rocks or stir decaying leaves and fruit.

Put the pill bugs under the wet paper towels. Give your pill bugs some food. They like leftovers. In nature, they are *scavengers*. They help to keep the earth clean. You can give them a few potato peelings, carrot peelings, lettuce leaves, or old garden leaves. Wash everything first to make certain it does not have any poison sprays on it. Do not overfeed them.

Now cover the container with the cardboard. The cardboard should have air-holes in it. Put a rock or something heavy on top of the cardboard so the pill bugs can't get out and make their home in your room.

Put the container in a cool place without too much light. If you keep the pill bugs comfortable, you can watch them grow. Pill bugs grow by shedding, or *molting*, their outside skin. You will find old skins in the container, if the pill bugs don't eat them first. The new skin is very shiny.

If you keep your pill bugs several months, the males and females may mate. It's not easy to tell them apart, but males are darker than females. The mother carries the babies around with her for about six weeks. She carries them in a special pouch under her body. After that, you may see them in the container. Baby pill bugs are very white and soft at first. They eat the same food as their parents. Pill bugs may live several years if nothing bothers them.

If this project is done at school, before summer vacation you should always put your pill bugs back out in the yard in a damp place near some rocks.

Pill bug feeding project

What type of food do pill bugs like best? Put damp rose petals and a damp lettuce leaf in your container. Which gets eaten first? Now put a fresh lettuce leaf and an old lettuce leaf in the container. Which gets eaten first? What about a fresh apple slice and an old apple slice? A peach pit? Can you find anything pill bugs won't eat?

What do you think would happen if there were no pill bugs or sow bugs in nature?

Information

There are about 80,000 kinds of snails. They live in oceans, deserts, forests, rivers, and many gardens. Garden snails do enormous damage to fruit, vegetables, and other plants. They eat just about any type of food product. You can test this out in your container.

Garden snails are related to clams and oysters, which live in water. Like them, they must have a living area that is damp and shady. During the daytime and dry weather, snails close up their shell "door." They seal it shut with "slime," or mucus, so they won't dry out. This is the same mucus they give off as a damp cushion when traveling.

What you need

1 a 1-gallon (3.8-liter) jar or plastic container

2 2 or 3 garden snails
Note: Some states have too many garden snails, other states don't have any and don't want any. If you live where there are lots of garden snails, this is a fine project. But don't carry any from one state to another. There are strict laws against this.

3 earth without lumps

4 a small clean can

5 some twigs or a small branch

6 water

Snails

What to do

Fill your jar about one-third full of earth. Put in a twig or two for the snails to climb on. Lay a small empty can sideways, burying it a little in the earth. This is a nice shady spot for the snails to hide in. Pour in ¹/₂ cup (125 milliliters) of water to dampen the earth.

Now add your snails. Cover the jar with something the snails won't eat, like several pieces of aluminum foil. Put a rubber band around this covering to hold it in place. Make small holes in the foil or other covering—snails must breathe air to survive.

Put the jar in a cool, shady place if you want your snails to move about in the daytime. Carefully pour ¹/₂ cup (125 milliliters) of water in the container whenever the earth starts to feel dry.

Feed your snails leftover lettuce leaves, orange peels, or potato peels. Feed them a little bit at a time. Add more food when the old food is gone. A snail has 21,000 sawlike teeth on its long tongue. It smells food with its two lower feelers, or *tentacles*. It eats quickly. Since snails need calcium to keep their shells strong and healthy, you want to add a piece of eggshell into the container about once a week.

If your snails are well kept, they may mate. A snail is both male and female. But it does need to join with another snail for a short time so each can lay healthy eggs. After mating, each snail digs a small hole in the earth with its foot. Into the hole go about 40 white rubbery eggs. A month later, baby snails come out. You might see this in your container if you are patient. A snail can live up to four years. The older a snail, the more shell whorls it has.

Snail projects

Collect empty snail shells from the garden. Can you find any with the same markings? Snail shells are like our fingerprints. No two are exactly alike.

Now put the empty shells in a row according to the number of whorls. Can you find what looks like a very old snail? The oldest snails have about five whorls.

Is there any food a snail won't eat? Try carrots, potatoes, or a tiny piece of meat. Why do you think farmers dislike snails?

Herb History, Folklore, and Growing Instructions

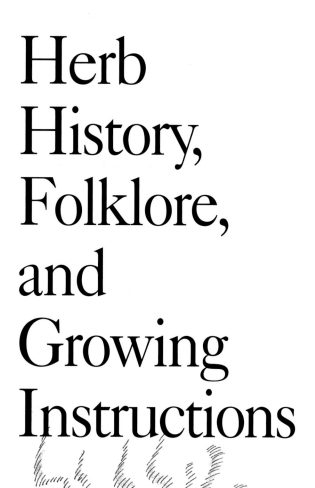

5

History of herbs

The first written records mentioning herbs date back to 3000 B.C. But herb use began long before that. Whether sweet smelling, spicy, or strong smelling, the aroma of herbs probably led early people to believe these plants had special powers of some kind. So far, our earliest definite proof of herb use is the discovery of wild marjoram pollen in dwelling caves dating back 60,000 years.

The beginnings of detailed written herb history is usually attributed to information coming from ancient Roman and Greek poetry and myths. These civilizations had many gods, each believed to be quite powerful. The people thought some herbs were gifts from the gods to help people cure their illnesses or take away their worries. Often herbs were burnt as incense in the hope that their sweet-smelling smoke would drift toward the heavens and make the gods happy. It was rare to find a household that didn't use herbs in some way in daily living.

For example, without refrigeration of any kind, food started to spoil quickly. What better way to disguise any smell than with aromatic herbs? Water wasn't always easily available, so many people didn't bathe often. Herbs and flowers were made into body perfumes, another smell disguiser. And without water to wash floors, herbs were scattered over the floors, too, making a more pleasant aroma.

Roman and Greek scholars gradually began the first formal herb studies. Lists were made of possible uses; medical, household, magic, or religious. When a problem came up, scholars and others could reference the list, trying to find the best herb, or herbs, to do the job. The modern word *herb* comes from the Latin word *herba*, meaning "grass."

By the first century A.D., a Roman doctor in Emperor Nero's army was able to list 600 plants having medicinal value. His book was called *De Materia Medica*. It was considered the basic herb text for 1,500 years.

As the Roman army spread out over conquered lands, its soldiers brought along both customs and information. Later, Roman administrators arrived, and with them came monks who brought not only religious beliefs but knowledge about plants. Herbs were often carried as gifts from one monastery to another by traveling monks.

When the Roman Empire began to fall apart, it was the monks who primarily continued herbal studies and use. Many monasteries had special gardens that contained only medicinal herbs.

Gradually, dispensing medicinal herbs became a business. Apothecaries, called druggists today, initially would go out and gather wild herbs. But this took a lot of time. So they began planting herbs near their homes. The word *drug* comes from the old Germanic word *drigan*, which means "to dry." The original drugs were dried herbs.

Apothecaries soon started planting their herbs for decoration as well as for practical use. The decorative idea spread to private homes, and soon most people had an herb garden. Although small homes had only medicinal herbs, the larger homes grew herbs for fragrance, cooking, and visual beauty. Herbs were the first plants used for garden landscaping.

There were many theories about herbal healing. One very popular school of thought in the sixteenth century was called the Doctrine of Signatures. This doctrine stated that a plant's color and shape were signs of how it should be used.

Yellow flowers, for example, were used in curing jaundice, a disorder in which the skin turns yellowish. A plant with wide balloonlike seed capsules might be used for curing swellings; a plant with heavy veins, similar to a snake's skin, would be used to cure snake bite; and so on. There were other herbal schools of thought, too; for example, certain herbs were related to the planets and zodiac signs and were used according to special formulas to cure illness.

When the first colonists came to North America, they carried herb seeds with them. They found that Native Americans also used herbs of many kinds to give food flavor, to prevent or cure disease, and to preserve dried meat. The colonists adopted many of these herbs, adding their own uses.

Herbs were only for personal use until the Shakers, a religious group, came to New York in 1776. As in early times, the Shakers gathered herbs, then began growing them close to home. Later, these plots became herb farms, and from there, herbs went out for sale.

Now every grocery carries herbs: fresh in the vegetable section, as an ingredient in canned or frozen foods, or in tea bags or dried seasonings.

Herbs are generally not used today for true medicinal purposes. Scientists have discovered proven effective cures for many disorders. Many people, however, still believe certain herbs have some health value.

History

According to long-ago storytellers, Basilik, king of dragon-snakes, had such strong breath that if it came near plants, it would destroy them. It could also kill humans with just one stare. How did the pretty basil herb possibly get named after this dreaded beast? No one quite knows.

There are many different types of basil, all with their history in the Far East. The very earliest varieties of this sweet-smelling herb were raised for use in religious ceremonies, but later it was adopted for cooking.

Throughout much of its early history, instructions for planting basil included stomping on the seeds and yelling insults at them. This was supposed to make the plant grow better.

It sounds silly, but one modern garden expert came up with a good enough explanation. Basil seeds are tiny, but even at this size they contain a jellylike material. Once the seeds are watered, such as when they are planted, the jelly or gelatin surrounds the seeds. At this point, the seeds might just float away.

Sweet Basil
Ocimum basilicum

How do you stop them from floating? Stamp them in well, of course. The old-time farmers may not have known the "why," but they knew how to get better results. You don't have to stamp on your basil seeds, but you can give them a solid push into the container earth with your thumb.

As an experiment, you can also yell at some seeds and not at others. See if there is any difference in how they grow. You can even set up a scientific experiment comparing the effects of singing, yelling, and storytelling.

How to grow

There are many different varieties of basil. Some grow quite large. For house-plant size, try bush basil. This plant can be kept to 3 inches (7.6 centimeters) high. The variety Spicy Globe is quite good for a windowsill. If you want basil with dark red leaves, Dark Opal grows to about 10 inches (25.4 centimeters) high. Try some of each.

You can use an old coffee cup or leakproof cup for your seeds. You may want to use a larger container, like a clean coffee can or plastic flowerpot, if you grow a larger variety of basil.

Fill the container two-thirds full of potting soil. Sprinkle basil seeds on top of the soil. Press the seeds down well, remembering the old folktale. Place your container by a sunny window. Water lightly until the earth is damp.

Seedlings appear in about ten days. Remember, the soil must be kept damp, but not wet. Let the plants grow for several weeks. Then remove some leaves. Give these leaves to an adult for use in salads. The extras can be frozen in a sandwich bag.

Uses for basil

You may want to try making basil vinegar if an adult will help you. Purple basil works best for vinegar. You need a glass jar with a lid. Fill the jar with basil leaves and stems. Pour in clear "white" vinegar. Put a piece of waxed paper over the jar top. Screw the lid on. Don't screw it on too tightly or it will stick.

Put the jar in a cabinet. If you look at it every day or so, you will see the vinegar turning purple. Strain out plant leaves and stems before using it on a salad.

An old-time use for basil was to keep flies out of the house. This was before window screens. Pots of basil were placed on windowsills and balconies. This is still done in some rural places in Europe. If you can find a way to test this, it is another interesting basil project.

156

History

In ancient Rome, about the fifth century, strong-tasting chives and other members of the onion group were fed to racehorses, wrestlers, and workers to make them strong. Because many people believed that a strong-tasting plant had greater healing power, tangy chives were believed to improve appetite, kidney function, and blood pressure, plus relieve sunburn pain and make a person's throat feel better during a cold.

The European explorer Marco Polo wrote about discovering chives when traveling through China in the late thirteenth century. Chives had been used by the Chinese for 3,000 years before Marco Polo ever saw them. This fantastic explorer brought some plants back to Europe with him, and from here chives soon were used in cooking throughout the world.

A couple of other uses were soon found. To prevent bad luck, chives were hung from house rafters. And if a gardener had moles eating his flowers, chives in the area were supposed to keep them away.

Chives
Allium schoenoprasum

How to grow

This is an easy herb to grow. Try garlic chives (*Allium tuberosum*) for starters, although regular chives grow nicely all year-round too.

Chives have a big root system, so containers should be at least 6 inches (15 centimeters) wide, about coffee can size. Fill the container two-thirds full of potting soil. Sprinkle seeds over the top. Cover lightly with soil. Sprinkle with water until the soil is damp but not wet.

Place the container in full sun if possible. Artificial light is fine, too. Seedlings appear in two weeks. They look like little grass blades. Thin the seedlings to a few inches apart so they have more room to grow. Always keep the soil slightly damp.

You can eat the seedlings you pull out, but wash off all dirt and remove the roots. The remaining chives will grow 8 to 12 inches (20 to 30 centimeters) tall. You can begin cutting the leaves when they are 2 inches (5 centimeters) tall. Start with the outside leaves first. Never remove all the leaves, or the plant won't grow.

If you let the chive plant grow for a year or so, you may see little lavender flowers starting in May. After the plant flowers, have an adult cut the grasslike leaves off midway. The plant will then do fine.

Uses for chives

Chives are used on potatoes, in salads, on bread, in all types of vegetable cooking. They contain vitamins A and C, so they're healthy, too. Eating chives will give you a strong onion breath, however. Some people eat parsley after they eat chives. It is supposed to help. This is an experiment you can design, if you can find somebody who wants to work with you.

History

Some people don't like the smell of coriander leaves. As a hint, the plant's name comes from the Greek word *koros*, or "bug." Some bugs, either while defending themselves or when squashed, give off a smelly fluid. But although coriander leaves may smell strong, the round seeds smell quite nice.

Coriander seeds have been found in ancient Egyptian tombs. When the Roman armies of Julius Caesar marched through Europe in about 50 B.C., they carried coriander seeds with them to flavor their food. They also used coriander to help prevent their meat from spoiling. Coriander's use spread, and eventually it came to America. Now the hardy coriander grows in gardens and in the wild.

Coriander
Coriandrum sativum

Before modern medicine, smelly coriander was tried as a cure-all for a variety of illnesses. In China, a coriander gargle was supposed to decrease toothache pain. In India, this herb was used to treat several eye problems. Stomachaches and gas pains were also on the medicinal list.

How to grow

Coriander is very easy to grow from seed. Use a container about 6 inches (15 centimeters) deep and 6 inches (15 centimeters) wide. A 1-pound (.5 kilogram) coffee can is a fine size. Fill the container two-thirds full of potting soil.

Sprinkle seeds onto the soil. Cover them ½ inch (1.3 centimeters) deep. Water gently just until the soil is damp. Now place the container by a sunny window.

Seedlings appear in one to three weeks. Remember to keep the soil slightly damp. Seedlings cannot survive drying out. When the stems reach two inches tall, take out the smaller ones. This gives more growing room for the others.

You can begin cutting coriander leaves when they are about 4 inches (10 centimeters) tall. Don't wait until the plant blooms, or the leaves become too tough.

If you grow the plant until it blooms, you will see its pretty light pink flower clusters. These plants have pink pollen, too. Some people put coriander in their outside gardens to attract bees. Bees like coriander. Bees collecting pollen from coriander carry pink pollen baskets instead of the usual yellow ones.

Uses for coriander

Coriander has two other names: *cilantro* and *Chinese parsley*. You may see it in the grocery stores under these names rather than *coriander*. Take a look.

Although the names may be unfamiliar, chances are if you have eaten Turkish, Indian, Mexican, or Chinese food, it has been flavored with coriander. This herb is even found in some hot dogs.

Coriander leaves contain vitamins A and C, plus calcium, phosphorus, iron, and some protein. In addition to flavoring food, it is used to disguise the taste of some prescription medicines.

History

The word *dill* comes from the old Norse word *dilla*. This means "to lull," or "help put to sleep." Dill tea was supposed to be a sleeping aid.

Perhaps your grandmother remembers this old English lullaby sung to babies for hundreds of years, including American babies. It goes, "Lavender blue, dilly dilly. Lavender green. When you are king, dilly dilly. I shall be queen."

The "dilly" in the lullaby refers to dill tea. Ask your grandmother if she knows that. She might have thought it was just a silly word. Most people do.

Magicians from long ago sometimes used dill as part of their secret formulas to cast spells. People who thought a magician might be casting a spell on them would make up a special drink that always included dill leaves. That was supposed to stop any problems before they started. To make doubly sure, the person would hang dill branches above the home entry door.

The early American colonists had a completely different use for the strong smelling, sweet-sour seeds, however. They chewed them during long church meetings to help them stay awake. Back in colonial days, if you heard the term "meeting seeds," they were talking about dill seeds.

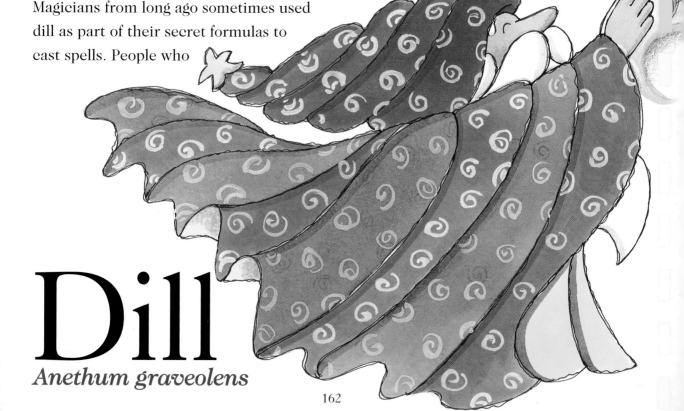

Dill
Anethum graveolens

potting soil. Water gently until the soil is slightly damp. Place the container in a sunny area.

Dill seedlings appear in about two weeks. When the plants reach 2 inches (5 centimeters) tall, remove all but the two biggest. Otherwise they get too crowded to grow well. As the plants grow, don't forget to water so the soil stays slightly damp, not wet.

Dill leaves are feathery. You can cut them just before the plants start to bloom. But you might want to leave one pot uncut. Dill has very pretty yellow flower clusters.

Uses for dill

If you've ever eaten a dill pickle, you've tasted dill. Dill pickles are special small cucumbers soaked in salted water with dill seeds added. Dill is also used to flavor rye and pumpernickel breads.

At home, you may want to place some feathery dill leaves on cooked potatoes and salads. It looks pretty. Smaller pieces of dill can be added to soup or scrambled eggs. This herb contains vitamin C, potassium, magnesium, iron, and calcium. You can have an adult watch while you cut the dill.

How to grow

Standard size dill can grow to 4 feet (1.2 meters) high, although indoors it stays shorter than that. Look for the dwarf form in your seed store. It grows to about 12 inches (30 centimeters) tall.

Fill a coffee can or container of similar size two-thirds full of potting soil. Start with about 6 dill seeds placed on the earth and then covered lightly with

History

Fennel was used by ancient Romans, Greeks, and Egyptians for both cooking and medicine. People continued to believe in the powers of licorice-smelling fennel throughout many centuries.

In Europe, fennel was hung from house rafters to keep away bad happenings and bring luck. Fennel seeds were placed in keyholes to keep ghosts from sneaking in. Plagued with fleas, housewives in the sixteenth century would sprinkle fennel over the house floors. Fleas were supposed to stay away from it. Also, without modern cleaning mops or running water, the licorice smell overcame the smell of household dirt.

Every area seemed to have its own uses for fennel. To keep from gulping food, people ate fennel. The thin leaves were supposed to make the eater equally thin. Fennel tea was used to ease stomach upsets. Fennel "bandages" were applied to cure snake bites, dog bites, toothaches, and earaches.

The American colonists brought fennel seeds along with them. Their use? A week of hard labor from sunup to sundown made people fall asleep easily. Smelling fennel leaves helped keep them awake during the long church sermons that were a basic part of colonial life. Every early garden had a fennel patch growing for just this purpose.

Fennel
Foeniculum vulgare

Fennel has become common in many vacant lots and fields. It is almost like a weed that smells like licorice. But never eat it or even taste it in the wild. There are other plants that smell like licorice, and these can make you quite sick.

How to grow

Some fennel plants can reach 6 feet (1.8 meters) tall. You want to buy seeds for the short variety. Bronze fennel grows to only about 15 inches (38 centimeters) high.

Use a 3-pound (1.5-kilogram) coffee can or similar size container. Fill it two-thirds full of potting soil. Sprinkle fennel seeds over the soil. Cover the seeds very lightly with more soil. Then add water gently.

Place the container by a sunny window. Keep the soil very slightly damp. Do not overwater. Fennel does best a bit on the dry side.

Seedlings appear in about two weeks. When the seedlings reach 3 inches (7.6 centimeters) tall, take out all but the biggest three. That prevents plant crowding. If any plant in the container starts getting too tall, cut off the center stem. You might want to let one fennel plant grow, to see the pretty yellow flower groups.

Uses for fennel

Fennel is often used in Italian cooking. Look up some recipes in a big cookbook. If you need fennel seeds, you can dry the ones that appear after flowering. Most recipes work best with seeds bought at the store, however. Uses for fennel leaves include putting them on top of pizza, adding them to soup, or decorating salads. Break off the leaves just before flowers bloom.

History

Legend has it that sweet-smelling majoram was created by the goddess Venus. Venus was in charge of love. Wreaths made of marjoram were placed on the heads of both the bride and the groom in ancient Rome and Greece. In addition, if marjoram was planted on a grave, the soul of the departed would be happy as long as the plant grew.

Long ago, before there were vacuum cleaners and other ways to clean houses, people scattered marjoram leaves on the floor. When people stepped on the small leaves, the sweet smell would come out and perfume the air.

Women also sometimes put marjoram leaves in their wash water, along with other sweet herbs, so their clothes would have a pretty smell.

Sweet Marjoram

Origanum majorana

How to grow

You can use a leakproof cup to hold a single small plant for a while. A 3-pound (1.5-kilogram) coffee can or similar size container works better because each marjoram plant can grow to 12 inches (30 centimeters) tall.

Fill the container two-thirds full of potting soil. Sprinkle seeds over the soil. Press the seeds in firmly with your thumb or palm. But don't press them in too deep.

Water until the soil is just damp. Place the container in a sunny place. Keep the soil damp but not wet. Seedlings will appear in about four weeks. As the plants grow, take out all but the strongest. This gives it plenty of room to grow.

Uses for marjoram

Marjoram contains vitamins A and C, plus protein. Marjoram is often used mixed with thyme, chives, parsley, and sweet basil. A favored use is in tomato dishes, such as spaghetti and lasagna.

In Greek, *oros* means "mountain," and *ganos* means "joy." On Greek hillsides, marjoram (*Origanum majorana*), the pretty "joy of the mountains," is very much admired.

History

In Greek mythology, there was a god named Pluto. He was king of Hades, or the underworld. Pluto was married to Persephone. But he fell in love with a beautiful young nymph named Minthe.

Persephone found out about this. She became very jealous. So she changed Minthe into a lowly herb easily stepped on. This was supposed to be mint, which grows in damp places and is often walked on.

Mint began its growing history in the Mediterranean area. Ancient Romans used it in their foods. They also wore it in wreaths about their heads so they would smell minty. Roman women also chewed a paste made of mint and honey. In the days before toothbrushes, this helped sweeten their breath. It also masked any smell of wine. At one time, women had to drink in secret. Wine was only fit for men and gods.

Roman armies carried mint across Europe. There it acquired names as *menthe de Notre Dame* in France, meaning "our Lady's mint," and *erba Santa Maria* in Italy, meaning "St. Mary's herb."

Our early colonists brought mint to America. Here it became popular added to a liquor drink called the *mint julep*. This drink originated in the South and quickly became popular elsewhere. When anti-liquor groups developed in the 1800s, some crusaders wanted to tear up every mint bed in the state of Virginia.

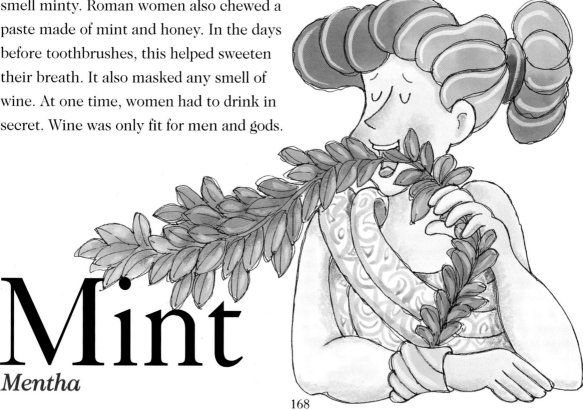

Mint
Mentha

Before modern medicine, mint was considered a very important plant in every herb doctor's pharmacy. Mint was used to treat watery eyes, bad memory, headaches, sore gums, gassy stomach, bad breath, bee stings, bad dreams, and dandruff. Mint does contain vitamins A and C, plus calcium and riboflavin. So it might have helped where a lack of vitamins was the basic problem.

Mint leaves, particularly peppermint, were used as toothbrushes. Mint was also added to bath water to make it sweet smelling. Leaves were scattered across bedrooms and dining rooms to leave a fresh scent. Mint had a double use. It was supposed to keep mice away.

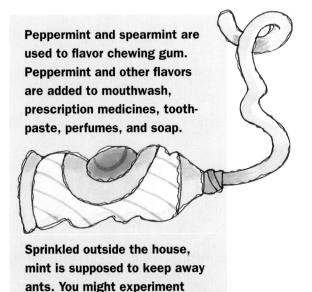

Peppermint and spearmint are used to flavor chewing gum. Peppermint and other flavors are added to mouthwash, prescription medicines, toothpaste, perfumes, and soap.

Sprinkled outside the house, mint is supposed to keep away ants. You might experiment with this if adults agree.

How to grow

There are over 25 commonly found mint varieties, each with its own special smell. Types include apple, orange, peppermint, pineapple, and spearmint. Try to find the small kinds for windowsill growth. Jewel mint grows only to an inch (2.5 centimeters) high. Orange mint grows to 8 inches (20 centimeters), but has the loveliest aroma.

Use a container at least 4 inches (10 centimeters) deep and 6 inches (15 centimeters) wide. Fill the container two-thirds full of potting soil. Sprinkle seeds on the soil and cover them lightly. Water gently until the soil is medium damp.

Unlike many herbs, mint does not have to be kept in bright light. In fact, it prefers a bit of shade. But do keep the soil very damp. Seedlings appear in about two weeks.

Uses for mint

Mint is added to fruit salads, vinegars, and mint sauces for meat. Growing mint is big business in the United States. Eighty percent of all commercial mint is produced here. The best growing grounds are drained swamps, so you can see that mint soil does really have to be keep somewhat wet.

History

Even today, some people wear a necklace containing a mustard seed charm at the end. The plant is mentioned in the New Testament. "If ye have faith as a grain of mustard seed . . ."

Mustard, both as a flavoring and medicine, goes far back into history. It reached England by way of the traveling Roman armies. In those days, before refrigerators of any kind, mustard seed was mixed with honey and vinegar. Then it was dried in the sun to keep it fresh.

In 1720, an English housewife discovered a way to grind mustard seeds into a pale yellow flour. This "flour" was mixed with cold water or grape juice to make a paste. This discovery was the beginning of today's mustard. You might try making some yourself. You'll see how the cold water or juice starts a chemical reaction on the mustard seeds. The true mustard smell takes about 15 minutes to appear.

Native American Indians used wild mustard seeds as a cure for nervousness. They also used mustard plasters and mustard baths. The spiciness of the mustard was supposed to help cure stuffy noses and the ordinary cold. Mustard plasters were used in your great-grandmother's day, and maybe in your grandmother's early childhood. Ask.

Mustard

Brassica species

How to grow

Mustard seeds are among the easiest herbs to grow. If you don't find them on the seed shelf of your garden store, look on the spice shelves of your local grocery or supermarket. Mustard seeds are large and easy to handle.

You can grow mustard in any container that is about 4 inches (10 centimeters) wide and 2 inches (5 centimeters) deep. Fill the container about halfway with potting soil. Water until the soil is quite damp. Then sprinkle the seeds fairly thickly on top. Place the container by a sunny window.

In about two days, you will see little green sprouts. In a week, you will have what looks like a green lawn. You can taste the leaves if you want. They are spicy. Some people like them. Some don't.

Uses for mustard greens

Sprinkle mustard greens on top of salads. Put them in sandwiches along with butter or margarine and garden cress for a healthy treat. Mustard greens are also prepared like spinach and served as a vegetable.

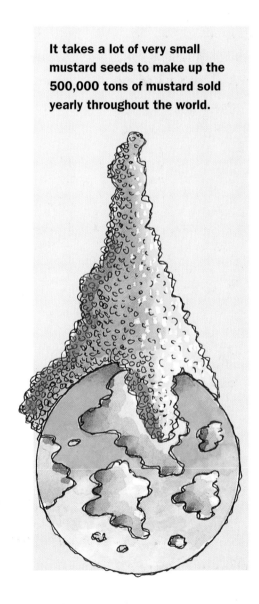

It takes a lot of very small mustard seeds to make up the 500,000 tons of mustard sold yearly throughout the world.

History

(see onions, page 84)

How to grow

Bunching onions, often known as *scallions* or *green onions*, grow nicely indoors from seed, unlike many other onions that are best planted from small bulbs bought at plant stores.

A clean cottage cheese container or similar size holder is fine. Fill the container about two-thirds full of potting soil. Sprinkle seeds on top and cover lightly. Place in a partially sunny or artificially lit area.

Skinny seedlings appear in two weeks. When plants are 3 inches (7.6 centimeters) high, thin to about an inch (2.5 centimeters) apart. When stems are pencil thick, an adult can begin clipping them to use for food.

Bunching Onions
Allium species

History

Parsley is one of the world's oldest herbs. It began its history in Europe. Nobody knows quite where.

The ancient Greeks made parsley wreaths and used them to crown winners of athletic games. Parsley wreaths were also placed around people's necks during banquets. This was supposed to stop them from drinking too much. Then, because banquet food often contained a lot of onions and garlic, diners would chew on parsley afterward. This sweetened their breath for awhile. Since this was before toothpaste, chewing on parsley also helped keep mouths clean.

In some long-ago cultures, parsley was associated with death. A legend tells that the entire Greek army once panicked and ran because an enemy sent a donkey covered with parsley into their midst.

Parsley is closely related to celery. Its ancient Greek name was *Petroselinon*. This later got shortened to *petersilie*, and later to the English *parcelye*.

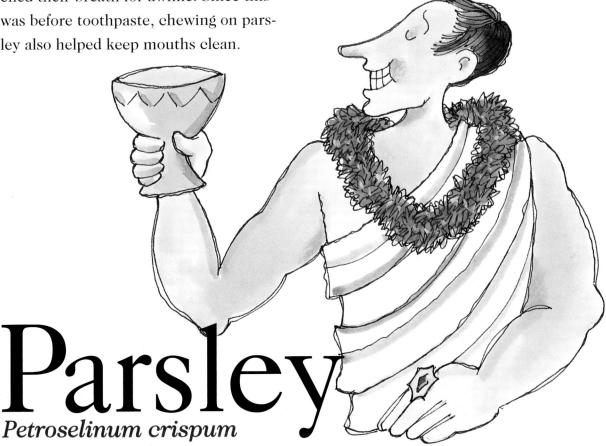

Parsley
Petroselinum crispum

There were many myths about parsley. Some people believed it only sprouted if planted by a good person. If it was planted by a good person who was expecting a baby, that was even better for parsley growth.

One was never supposed to bring parsley from one home to another. That was bad luck. Many people still refuse to transplant parsley because they believe it brings bad luck. In gardening, parsley does not transplant well because of its long taproot. The message people got from this information may have translated to poor growth and then bad luck.

Parsley was in the medical herbalist's remedy container. Eating wild parsley was supposed to cure kidney stones. If you had a gassy stomach, parsley soaked in water would help. Skin problems, bruises, rheumatism, and back pain were all thought to be helped by parsley.

Nor were farm animals forgotten. Parsley was supposed to cure sick sheep. Parsley contains iron, magnesium, potassium, and B vitamins. It is an excellent source of vitamin A and, on an equal weight basis, has three times more vitamin C than an orange.

How to grow

A 6-inch (15-centimeter) wide pot can hold five dwarf parsley plants if you don't mind them a bit crowded. The pot should be at least 4 inches (10 centimeters) deep.

Soak the seeds for 12 to 24 hours before planting. As an experiment, you can see if the longer soaking time helps sprouting. Parsley plants do take a long time to appear, sometimes as long as six weeks. For this reason, it is not the easiest herb to grow. But it is fun to try.

Keep the container in a medium sunny area or under bright lamp light. The soil must be kept slightly damp. Depending on the type you plant, your parsley will grow from 6 to 12 inches (15 to 30 centimeters) high.

Cut the outside leaves only. The inner leaves will keep growing. Do not let flower spikes form. If they do, the leaves become bitter tasting.

Uses for parsley

In recent years, parsley has seen renewed use as a health food. People drink parsley juice and eat parsley, cress, and sprout sandwiches. Parsley is used fresh on salads, and is put into soup and other foods. It also is used to decorate food platters.

You can dry parsley in your refrigerator. Put it in a single layer on a dish. It takes about two weeks to dry completely.

Parsley stems were once ground into a powder and used as a dye. You can try this in the classroom or with an adult at home.

History

The ancient Romans considered rosemary a sacred herb and believed it brought happiness. They braided it into hair wreaths for special occasions, such as weddings. Sleeping on a rosemary pillow helped nervousness and was supposed to cure headaches.

Greek students braided rosemary sprigs into their hair every day. They thought the sweet aroma would help them remember the facts needed on tests. Later on, rosemary became associated with remembrance. A cup of rosemary tea was supposed to help both mind and memory.

An old custom, still followed in some places even today, is adding rosemary to a bride's bouquet to mark the passing from one loving family to another. At the same time, the groom gets a little rosemary nosegay bound with gold ribbon. This is a reminder that he should be faithful.

In one version of the story "The Sleeping Beauty," the princess was surrounded by a hedge of thorny roses. To wake her up, she had to be touched by rosemary.

Rosemary
Rosmarinus officinalis

How to grow

Use a coffee can size container. Fill it two-thirds full with potting soil. Sprinkle with a lot of seed because only a small amount will sprout. Cover seeds lightly. You might try several different types of rosemary in different containers.

Water gently until the soil is just damp. Place the container in medium sunlight or under a lamp. The seedlings appear in three weeks, a long time. If the leaves start turning yellow, give the plants more light.

Rosemary grows slowly. Never overwater or let it dry out, or it will die. Your plant will reach between 10 inches to 3 feet (25.4 centimeters to 0.9 meter) high, depending on what type of seeds you used. Read the seed package for height. If you let it grow long enough, you will see pretty blue flowers.

Rosemary has sky blue flowers. Its Latin name *Rosmarinus* means "dew of the sea."

Uses for rosemary

Clip the pretty pine-smelling leaves to send in letters at Christmas. Give small plants to friends as happy memories. You might work with an adult to make a hair rinse. Use 1 ounce (29 grams) of dried rosemary leaves and flowers. Place in a saucepan and have an adult cover it with a pint (.5 liters) of boiling water. Let cool in a safe place. Use. Rosemary is still part of many hair preparations because of its nice aroma.

History

Sage has a long history of medical uses. Its scientific name Salvia comes from the Latin word salvere, which means "to save."

The ancient Romans thought sage was a sacred herb. It had to be collected in a special ceremony. Before anything was done, the gathering person had to offer bread and wine to the growing grounds. Then that person had to put on an all white outfit. Because all gathering had to be done barefoot, the person also had to have very clean feet before entering the garden.

Depending on the country, the 700 types of sage had many uses. In the Middle East, eating sage with meals was supposed to lead to increased intelligence. In some parts of Europe, it was believed that eating sage stopped poison snakes from biting.

In 1773 colonial America, the colonists finally decided not to pay the huge taxes put on imported tea from Britain. They dumped 342 chests of tea into Boston Harbor, now remembered as the Boston Tea Party. The British thought the colonists couldn't do without their tea. But they could. Sage tea became a popular substitute.

Sage
Salvia officinalis

How to grow

Use a coffee can size container. Fill two-thirds full of potting soil. Sprinkle seeds on top and cover lightly with soil. Press firmly on the soil. Water gently until slightly damp. Place the container near a sunny window.

Seedlings appear in two to three weeks. Depending on the type of sage, you may have plants reaching from 6 inches to 3 feet (15 centimeters to 0.9 meter) high. Read the instructions on the seed packet before you buy it to be sure you buy dwarf or short plants for indoor use.

You may want to try pineapple sage just for its lovely pineapple smell. This sage also has bright red flowers if full grown by late spring. Pick the leaves before the plant blooms.

Uses for sage

Put sage leaves on top of chicken or pork roast while cooking to give a lovely flavor. Sage is also used for fragrance around the home and as a dye.

History

According to legend, thyme came into being when tears from the beautiful Helen of Troy hit the ground. The ancient Greeks thought thyme perfume brought back energy. It smelled so sweet that servant women used it in their wash water.

If thyme was burned, according to ancient Roman teachers, all poisonous insects and animals were supposed to leave the area. It was offered up on altars to various gods by both the Greeks and the Romans. The ancient Egyptians placed thyme around their mummies.

In Europe, thyme was placed in linens to give them a sweet aroma. It also was supposed to protect materials from insect damage. Herb doctors used thyme to cure bad moods, flu, gas, and hair loss.

When knights and ladies-in-waiting were plentiful, the ladies often had to do a lot of waiting for their heroes to return home from battle. To occupy themselves, they embroidered thyme pictures on silken scarves. A bee would be flying around the thyme. This was a double symbol for activity. Thyme equaled courage. And the scarves were given to the knights to wear in future battles.

Long ago, when more people than now believed in fairies and elves, it was believed that the wee folk made their home in thyme. During the fifteenth-century Renaissance period in Europe, if you drank thyme tea in a special potion, you were supposed to be able to see these fairies. If you could see them, you could make certain they didn't do you any mischief.

Thyme

Thymus vulgaris

How to grow

There are many different types of thyme. Read the seed packages to see which grow to less than 8 inches (20 centimeters), a nice indoor size. There are also creeping thymes that stay very close to the ground.

Use a coffee can size container, or a large deep bowl. Fill two-thirds full of potting soil. Sprinkle seeds on top and cover lightly. Water gently until just slightly damp. Do not overwater.

Keep the container in a quite sunny window. Seedlings appear in about three to four weeks. They are reddish colored. You can cut leaves or sprigs at any time. If you let some sections grow uncut, you may see white flowers in summer.

Uses for thyme

Thyme is a quite strong herb. Use a little bit in soups and in chicken and turkey stuffings. Thymol, an oil taken from some types of thyme, is still used in some commercial cough medicines.

Thyme, in the language of flowers, is supposed to mean courage and activity.

Easy Plant Craft Projects

Whereas some craft projects require your total concentration to get the best results, many can be accomplished while watching television or listening to music. If you become quite good at making pomander balls, cornhusk dolls, holiday wreaths, or any other pretty project, you may even be able to offer it at school fund-raising fairs. Certainly you will never lack for gifts to give friends, family, neighbors, or classmates for birthdays or other celebrations.

Flower craft projects can be done alone, in a group of friends, or with family members. You can do flower craft projects any day of the year, but sometimes it's even more fun on a rainy or snowy winter day when you have to stay indoors.

6

New World settlers brought their Old World European flower-drying habits with them. Flowers throughout the year helped brighten small hand-built homes, and cheered often lonely and dangerous winters. During spring and summer, even the youngest children helped collect those blossoms that kept much of their shape and color when dried. These included strawflowers, statice, cockscomb, roses, dahlias, everlastings, lavenders, lunaria, fennel, globe thistle, and globe amaranth.

Household women and children would tie about five stems loosely together for most flowers. The tied stem bottoms were attached to a piece of string. Then the flowers were hung upside down from hooks in dry, dark attics or basements. The air would dry them so they almost looked as if they were still alive.

What to do

You can try this same technique today by tying five dryable flower stems to coat hangers. You can use a rubber band rather than string to make the grouping. If using roses, tie them singly rather than in groups. Hang the flowers upside down in a closet or dark, dry room. The darkness is necessary to help keep the flower color from fading. Room dryness prevents mildew from disfiguring the flowers and leaves. Do not let plant bunches touch each other.

Plan on about a ten-day drying time. You can test for dryness by snapping a stem. If it snaps easily, the plant is dry. You can leave plants hanging until ready to use, or place carefully in covered boxes.

If you want the closest match to the orginal shading, use light-colored flowers. Darker ones tend to fade. Pick all flowers when the outside air is dry, around noon, rather than when it is damp, as in the morning. Use flowers that have begun to open. Buds do not air dry as well. Never place anything you've cut for drying in water, as you might if you were planning a fresh vase arrangement.

Air drying flowers

What you need

1 autumn leaves in several colors and shapes

2 an old newspaper

3 corrugated cardboard

4 a box of books or other heavy weight

Drying autumn leaves

Early settler homes were often surrounded by forest, and autumn leaves were too beautiful to resist. So they were dried and used indoors. You can do this, too.

What to do

Collect colorful autumn leaves. Put a large piece of corrugated cardboard on the floor or other flat place so the leaves dry flat. Place five thicknesses of newspaper over the cardboard. Now place the leaves on the newspaper. The leaves should not be touching.

Cover the leaves with five sheets of newspaper. Press down with heavy books, bricks, or a box filled with stones. Let it dry for three weeks.

How to use

If you have collected leaves with stems attached, they look lovely in vases. Or you may want to make a leaf picture. Use a large sheet of white or colored paper and white glue. You can glue leaves on top of each other for a three-dimensional effect. Let it dry well before moving.

You may want to experiment with absorption plant drying in addition to air drying. Here you place the plants in a box filled with a mixture of borax, borax and cornmeal, kitty litter, purchased clean sand, or silica gel. The purpose of any of these ingredients is to get rid of the dampness in fresh flowers.

Cat litter blot drying

What you need

1 an unopened bag of cat box litter

2 a sturdy box (shoebox)

3 herbs and/or flowers including roses, butterfly bush, chrysanthemums, dandelions, daisies, marigolds, dahlias, zinnias, or sunflowers

What to do

Line the box with three layers of newspaper. Place 2 inches (5 centimeters) of litter in the box. Pick flowers as soon as they open. Inspect them first. You need perfectly shaped flowers for this to work well. Light-colored flowers are best because they hold color better.

Blot drying plants

Pick all flowers when the outside air is dry, around noon, rather than when it is damp, as in the morning. Use flowers that have begun to open. Buds do not dry as well because the trapped moisture tends to turn them brown.

Never place anything you've cut for drying in water, as you might if planning a fresh vase arrangement.

Cut stems to about 5 inches (12.7 centimeters). Remove leaves you won't want. Set flowers lengthwise on the litter. They should be facing down. Flowers should not touch each other.

Lightly sprinkle 1 inch (2.5 centimeters) of litter over the flowers and around them. Continue sprinkling until the flowers are completely covered. Allow to dry for a week. Do not cover the container. Flowers removed before they are totally dry will wilt quickly.

When you remove flowers, be really careful. They may break. That's another reason to start with more flowers than you think you will need. Brush off any litter particles with an artist's watercolor or other skinny brush.

Alternate blotting material

The previous instructions can also be used with a cornmeal mixture and with very clean builder's sand. Modern craft stores sell silica gel for drying flowers. Obtain an instruction booklet with the gel.

All the ingredients for a basic old-time recipe for the cornmeal mixture are found in today's supermarkets. Have an adult assist you with mixing 5 pounds (2.3 kilograms) of cornmeal with a large package of borax, about 25 ounces (700 grams), and 1/4 cup (60 milliliters) of non-iodized salt. Blend thoroughly. Follow the same procedure as given for clean kitty litter.

Uses for dried flowers

The flowers can be used for small or large bouquets around the house or to decorate gifts.

What you need

1 4- by 8-inch (10- by 20-centimeter) pieces of clean white cotton or linen fabric

2 dried herb leaves

3 a needle and thread

What to do

Sew up the fabric like a pillowcase, leaving an opening on one side. Fill full of fragrant herbs, such as mint leaves, rosemary, sage, or thyme. Sew the bag's open end closed.

How to use

Drop into bath water to make it smell nice. You can make quite a few bags at a time. Store them in an airtight container.

Herbal bath water

In early America, and even up to your great-grandmother's time, these handmade bouquets, called "tussy mussys," were commonly seen. Then, as now, they were gifts for a friend, dinner table decorations, or even bouquets held by flower girls during wedding ceremonies.

What you need

1 a small lacy paper doily

2 aluminum foil

3 herb cuttings

4 ribbon

What to do

Make 4-inch (10-centimeter) long cuttings of pretty-smelling herbs. Some nice herbs for this project are thyme, sage, rosemary, and mint. If you can add one or two small fresh flowers, or dried flowers, to the bouquet, it adds a lovely spark of color.

Dampen the plant stems. Now neatly wrap a small square of aluminum foil around the stems. Use just enough to cover the stems completely. Poke the wrapped stems through the doily center. You may want to have an adult cut a little hole in the doily to make poking easier.

Scrunch the foil up under the doily so it stays in place. Now tie a pretty ribbon around the bouquet bottom.

Herb bouquet

What you need

1 corncob (kernels removed)

2 glue

3 fabric scraps

4 pipe cleaners

5 a needle and thread

6 a small empty spool of thread

What to do

The corncob must be very dry. Let it dry for a week in the sun, turning it every day. When the cob is dry, wrap two pipe cleaners around the top to make arms. Using two pipe cleaners gives the doll strong arms.

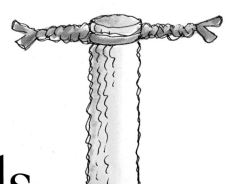

Corncob dolls

Glue the spool onto the top of the cob. Let it dry at least two hours. Now have an adult help you cut two pieces of fabric about 3 inches (7.6 centimeters) wide and about 6 inches (15 centimeters) long. Place these pieces on either side of the doll, and sew them together at the shoulders. The doll's head should stick out.

Now sew under the arms. You can sew all the way down if you want to. Tie a different color material around the doll's waist for a belt. You can use a ribbon if you want.

With a ballpoint pen or colored felt-tip pen, make a face on the spool. Early settlers used corn silk for hair. You can do this, too, or make hair from yarn or fabric. Glue it on. Cover the hair with a fabric scarf if you wish.

Designing corncob dolls was a favorite evening pastime during early American settler days. Corn was a basic food, so there were lots of cobs.

P ioneer children always had dolls, even if they had to make them. You can make cornhusk or corn-shuck dolls just as they did.

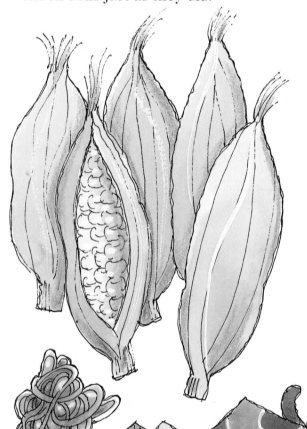

What you need

1 5 ears of fresh corn with green outer leaves (the husks)

2 rubber bands

3 small cloth scraps

4 yarn scraps

5 rubber cement or white glue

What to do

You will need about 10 to 14 husks. If corn isn't in season, you can buy the husks at stores that carry special Mexican groceries. The husks are used to make tamales.

Cornhusk dolls

Remove the husks from the corn. Separate the husks. Have an adult cut the bottom crinkled portion so they will lay flat. Place the husks in a sunny place to dry for about five days. Or you can put them between several sheets of paper toweling until dry. You can even put them between the pages of an old phone book. This helps hold them to a nice flat shape.

Have an adult watch while you cut the husk top edges so they aren't ragged. Now soak the husks in warm water for ten minutes until they become soft. Put the husks on paper towels or newspaper to soak up dripping water. Make a layer of five long husks. Now wrap a rubber band tightly around the top of your husk grouping. The rubber band should be about 1½ inches (3.8 centimeters) from the top. Using colored rubber bands is prettier than plain ones. Now double over the top part and tuck the ends under the rubber band. You have now made the doll's head.

Now roll two of the shorter husks together lengthwise. This roll should be very tight. Place rubber bands tightly at each end, about ½ inch (1.3 centimeters) from the end. You have just made the doll's arms and hands.

Slip the arms through the husks under the neck. Now tie yarn tightly around the doll's waist, or place a rubber band around the doll's waist. This holds the arms in place. With an adult's help, trim the bottom of the doll's husk dress.

You can make a doll's face with seeds or paint. You can design an outfit with fabric scraps, gluing them onto the husk. For hair, use corn silk as the pioneers did, or use yarn.

If you want a boy doll, cut the husk bottom to form legs. Put a rubber band around the bottom of each leg to hold it in place.

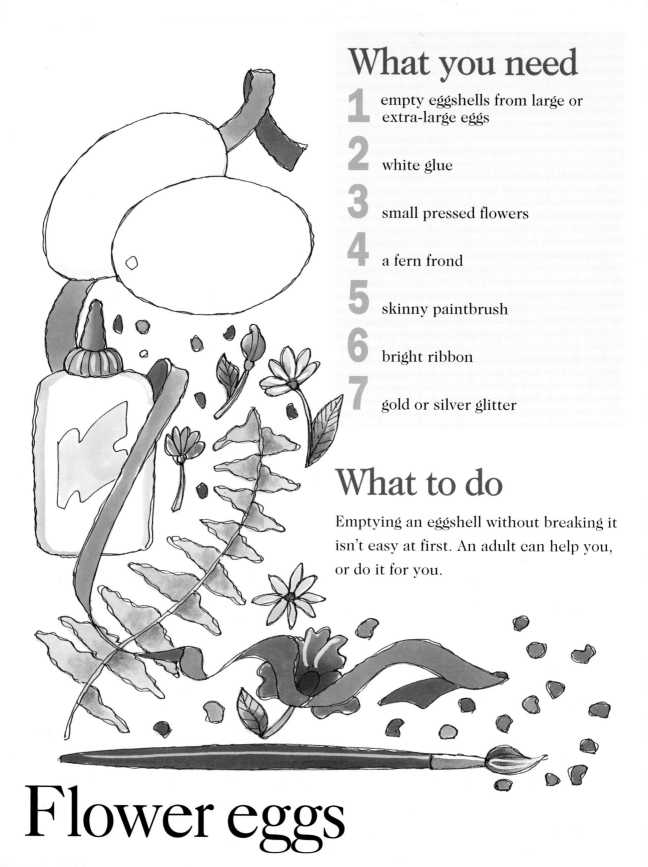

What you need

1. empty eggshells from large or extra-large eggs

2. white glue

3. small pressed flowers

4. a fern frond

5. skinny paintbrush

6. bright ribbon

7. gold or silver glitter

What to do

Emptying an eggshell without breaking it isn't easy at first. An adult can help you, or do it for you.

Flower eggs

Let the egg sit outside the refrigerator for about an hour. Shake the egg gently four times to loosen the insides. Then, poke a small hole in the egg top. Put a long, clean toothpick or other clean narrow poking stick into the hole, and gently mix the egg white and yolk within the egg.

Pour this mix out into the sink through the egg hole opening, or save to make scrambled eggs or use in baking. Rinse the empty eggshell with cold water. Let it dry overnight.

Dab some glue on the egg. Stick the pressed flowers onto the egg. Add some fern here and there to make leaves. Then glue some pretty ribbon around the egg. This hides the hole, and also makes a loop hanger.

You can make a bow for the top, and glue it on. You can sprinkle the egg with gold or silver glitter, too. Then let it dry overnight. Remember, you are dealing with eggshells. They will crack if handled too roughly.

What to do

Make holes in the Styrofoam with a fork. Don't make the holes too deep. About ⅓ inch (.8 centimeters) deep is fine; otherwise the flower stems will fall out. Put glue on a narrow bright ribbon. Wrap the ribbon around and across the ball. Let it dry, then tie to make a hanging loop.

Have an adult help you cut the dried flower stems to about ½ inch (1.3 centimeters) long. Dip the cut stems in white glue. Stick flowers with their glued stems into the Styrofoam ball holes. Cover the ball completely with the flowers. You can make a design, such as stripes or dots. Or you can just put the flower colors every which way and get a very pretty mixture.

What you need

1   a Styrofoam ball

2   dried flowers with short stems

3   white glue

How to use

Flower balls make good holiday, wedding, and birthday decorations.

Flower balls

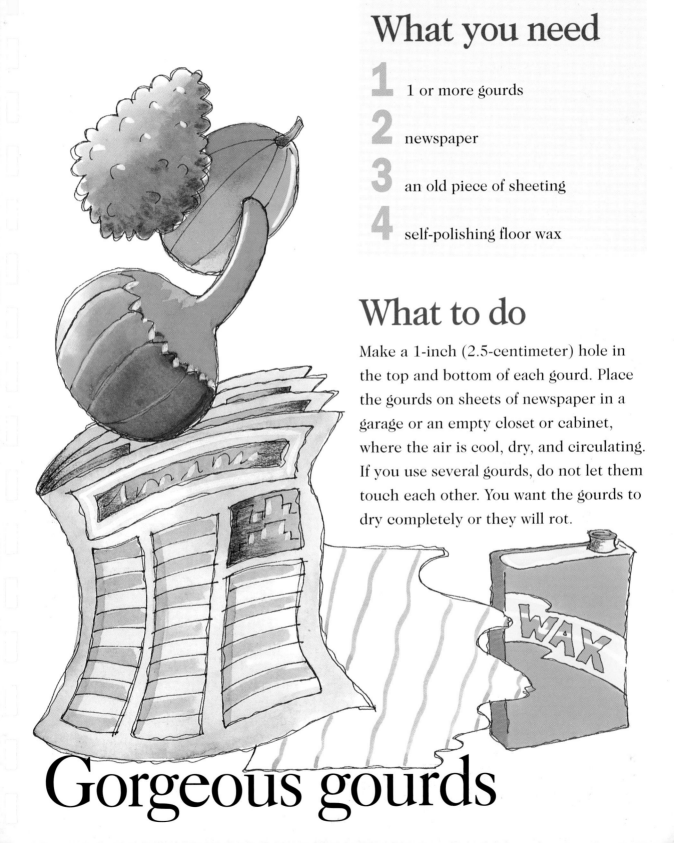

What you need

1 1 or more gourds

2 newspaper

3 an old piece of sheeting

4 self-polishing floor wax

What to do

Make a 1-inch (2.5-centimeter) hole in the top and bottom of each gourd. Place the gourds on sheets of newspaper in a garage or an empty closet or cabinet, where the air is cool, dry, and circulating. If you use several gourds, do not let them touch each other. You want the gourds to dry completely or they will rot.

WAX

Gorgeous gourds

Once a day, preferably in the morning, use an old piece of sheeting to wipe each gourd dry. Do this for about two weeks, turning the gourds to a new position each time. Then let the gourds dry another two weeks. When you shake a gourd, the seeds inside should rattle. That way you know it is dry. You may have to wait a few more weeks with a big gourd.

Wash the gourds with warm water and soap. If an adult will be cutting the gourds into a birdhouse, vase, or other shape, now is the right time. After cutting, paint the outside with self-polishing floor wax. Let it dry overnight.

How to use

Place several different colored gourds in a large bowl for decoration. Or you can push a piece of wire through the top and bottom hole. Leave several extra inches. Join the wire ends together. Now create a separate loop at each end. Use one loop to hang the gourds as a ornament. Put a ribbon bow through the other loop to make it even fancier.

Gourds are vegetables, relatives of the pumpkin and squash, but they are not for eating. Gourds are now used for decoration and birdhouses. In early societies, they were used to make eating bowls.

If you have a sunny, outdoor garden space, gourds are easy to grow. Otherwise you may be able to buy them at the supermarket around Thanksgiving, or at farm stands.

What you need

1 a glass container with a tight cover (jam or olive jar)

2 corn oil

3 herb leaves from thyme, marjoram, mint, rosemary, or any other well-scented leaves, *or* allspice, cinnamon sticks, or cloves

4 a strainer with small holes

What to do

Fill the container with herb leaves or spice. Add enough corn oil to cover the leaves or spice. Let it sit for 24 hours in a warm, sunny place. Strain the oil and herbs. Throw away the old herbs and add new herbs to the jar. Pour the used oil on top of the new herbs.

Perfumed oil

Do this every day for a week. By now your oil will have a pretty smell. If you want a stronger aroma, do this every day for another week.

How to use

You have created a perfumed oil. When finished, strain it one last time. Then pour it into little jars. Screw on jar covers tightly. You can use this oil if you make potpourri (see page 204). Or you can give it as a gift to someone who makes candles or soaps.

The aroma will not last as long as the perfumed oils found in stores. If you want the aroma to last a long time, perhaps an adult can buy you some perfume fixative from a large pharmacy, craft shop, or mail-order supplier.

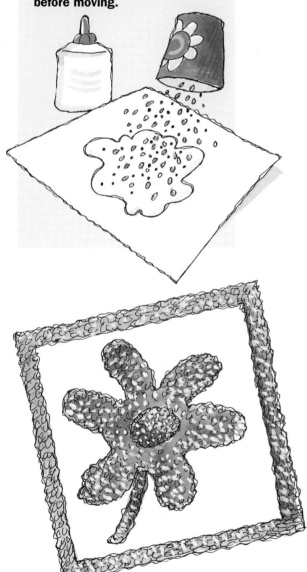

A hint: If you have a large area to fill in, brush on white glue. Then shake mustard seeds or dark poppy seeds from the container onto the glued cardboard. Always let it dry well before moving.

What you need

1 seeds of all kinds: sunflower, pumpkin, peanut, gourd, split pea, turnip, rice, radish, popcorn, squash, flower

2 large square piece of white or gray cardboard

3 white glue

What to do

Draw a picture on the cardboard. You can trace it from a book if you want. Then copy it onto the cardboard.

Paint a line of glue around the cardboard near the outside edge. This will be the picture frame. Place seeds on the glued area. The frame looks nicest if you use only one or two types of seeds rather than a mixture. Let this dry overnight. Then turn the cardboard over and tap it. Any loose seeds will fall off. Reglue them.

Now glue seeds on your design. Let it dry overnight. Turn the cardboard over. Tap it. Reglue any loose seeds that fall off.

Seed pictures

What you need

What to do

Poke shallow holes in the orange with the fork. Poke the fork this way and that rather than in a row, which could cause the orange to break along a line.

Press a clove in each hole with your finger. Try to cover the whole orange with cloves. Where the fork won't fit, use the toothpick to make a small hole—not too big or deep, or the clove will sink in and disappear. The clove is supposed to stay on the outside.

Pomander ball

When you are finished, the cloves should be in the fruit as thickly as possible. The less orange skin you can see, the better the pomander looks. When you have put in as many cloves as you can, sprinkle the pomander ball with pumpkin pie spice or allspice. If you have a hairpin, you can poke it into the center of the fruit. Leave a little bump up for a hanging ribbon tie.

Let the orange dry in a sunny, airy spot for at least two weeks. Turn it if necessary so all areas are exposed to the air. While drying, the orange skin shrinks. The orange will feel like a rock when ready for use. This holds the cloves firmly in place.

If you didn't use a hairpin, at this stage you can tie a blue, purple, or red ribbon around the pomander ball. The tie should have a little loop portion so you can dangle the ball on a hanger.

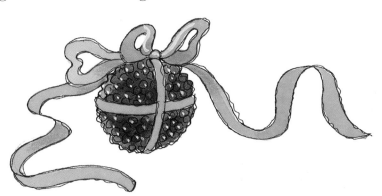

How to use

Pomander balls are often used to make closets smell nice. But you can make them as Christmas tree ornaments, too! Keep them in a plastic sandwich bag until ready for use. You can decorate the bag with glitter and ribbon as part of a gift.

The pomander has been used to scent closets since the Elizabethan era. The word *pomme* means "apple" in French. Originally pomanders were made with an apple base. The custom traveled to the United States. With the beginning of rail transportation, people began making pomanders out of the longer-lasting orange, lemon, lime, or grapefruit.

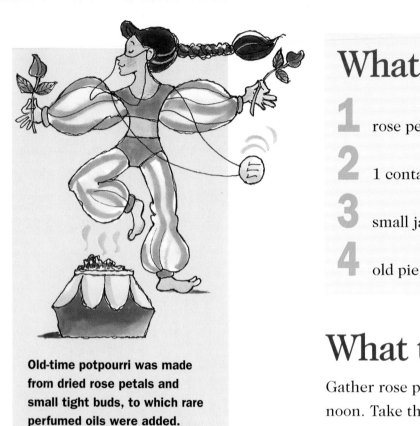

Old-time potpourri was made from dried rose petals and small tight buds, to which rare perfumed oils were added. Although this method is still used occasionally, it is easier to use rose petals only. Allspice, a common kitchen spice, is used in place of expensive perfumed oils.

What you need

1 rose petals from fragrant roses

2 1 container of allspice

3 small jars with lids

4 old pie tins

What to do

Gather rose petals on a hot dry afternoon. Take the petals off the flowers. Put them in the pie tins or other containers to dry. You can also place them on an old window screen, but keep the screen off the ground. Don't pile the petals too thickly.

Potpourri

Let the petals dry in a garage or other place away from light. Mix them at least once a day, otherwise you may get mold where two petals press against each other.

When all petals feel dry to the touch, but not crumbly, add 1 tablespoon of allspice. You can also add some cinnamon or cloves. Or you can add some herb leaves: mint, sage, or rosemary. Mix well with a wooden spoon or with your hands. Now scoop the petals into the jars. Screw lids on tightly.

How to use

You can decorate the jars with ribbon or cutouts from magazines. When you want to make a room smell nice, open the jar for awhile. If you keep the jar open all the time, the scent won't last very long. Make several jars at once, so you have a long-term supply.

You can also make gift sachets. Get leftover cotton material or small-hole netting. Make 6-inch (15-centimeter) squares. Crumble some potpourri in the middle.

Gather the material around the potpourri. Fasten the little bag with a rubber band. Now put a colorful ribbon around the rubber band, and tie the ribbon in a bow. Add a center string so people can hang it in the closet.

In colonial America, sentimental early settlers pressed their favorite flowers and loveliest leaves between book pages. If you ever find one of their old books on display, you may find a flower in it, too. But flower dampness is tough on books, so today we do the job with newspaper or blotting paper.

What you need

1 newspaper or blotting paper

2 corrugated cardboard

3 flowers and leaves

4 wax paper

5 a tweezers

6 a wooden board

7 white glue

What to do

Pressing flowers is best done in springtime, when there are many flower choices. But you may be able to do it any time of the year, depending on where you live.

Find pretty leaves and flowers without any spots or holes. You don't need too many to start with.

Pressed flowers

Set the corrugated cardboard on top of the wooden board. Place several sheets of newspaper or a sheet of blotting paper on top of the cardboard. Now set a white paper towel on top of the newspaper. Some newspaper has ink that comes off.

Take apart the larger flowers, such as the rose. Lay the petals, not touching, on the paper. If you have small flowers, such as pansies, you can place them face down and whole. Put some pretty green and gray leaves on the paper too. Make certain none of the plants touch each other or they won't dry properly.

Cover the flowers with several sheets of newspaper or a sheet of blotting paper. Place a piece of corrugated cardboard on top of this. Move the board carefully to someplace where it won't be disturbed for about a month. A garage is fine. Place books, bricks, or another heavy item on top of the paper. This acts as a press for the flowers.

At the end of about three weeks, the pressed petals and leaves should appear crisp. If they aren't, wait another two weeks.

Then use a tweezers to lift off the pressed flowers and leaves very carefully.

Place each petal and leaf on a sheet of waxed paper. When you are through, cover with another sheet of waxed paper. Store until you are ready to make designs.

How to use

Begin with plain white typing paper or plain note cards from the stationery store. Using small amounts of white glue, set each petal or leaf in place to make a design. The petals must be handled with great care. Using a tweezers is better than using your fingers.

If the petals or leaves seem too breakable, put the glue on the paper. Let it sit until slightly dry. Then with a damp fingertip, touch the flower, pick it up with your fingertip, and place it on the glued surface. Wash your hands afterward.

Allow the paper to dry. Now you have a picture for your grandmother or a favorite friend.

What to do

Have an adult help you cut a round circle in the middle of your paper plate. The circle does not have to be perfect. This circle is your wreath base.

Put some rubber cement around the outside rim of your wreath. Rubber cement is better than glue because it does not dry right away. If you use glue, just do a small section at a time.

Place bean seeds of all the same color in a row around the outside of your wreath. Now draw a design on the plate inside. You can copy a design from a book, or make up your own.

Using dabs of rubber cement, glue on melon seeds and bean seeds. Fill the entire inside. Then let your wreath dry overnight. Test to see if the beans fall off by gently tilting the wreath upward. Reglue any beans that fall off. Let it dry.

Make a small hole in the wreath top. Thread a ribbon through it. Now you can hang your wreath on the wall.

What you need

1 a heavy-duty paper plate

2 dried bean seeds of different colors

3 melon seeds of different kinds

4 rubber cement

5 a scissors

6 ribbon

Seed wreath

What to do

Cut the apple crosswise. The seeds inside form a star pattern. Pour a thin layer of each color paint into a separate container. Brush the paint lightly onto an apple half. Touch the painted side of the apple on the paper. Make your design.

You can add leaf prints by brushing paint very lightly onto the backs of various size garden leaves. Gently put the painted side of the leaf flat on the paper, then carefully lift it up without smudging. Be careful not to get paint on your clothes. Let the paper dry before you pick it up.

What you need

1 a small apple

2 plant leaves

3 finger paint of different colors

4 a paintbrush

5 white paper

6 old pie tins or cardboard meat holders

7 newspaper

8 an apron

How to use

Once you get experience making designs, you can use cut pieces of celery or carrot, or lemon halves to make different patterns. Use the designs as greeting cards or gift paintings. For a bigger gift project, use brown paper shopping bags.

Fruit stamp decoration

What to do

Styrofoam is fun to work with. Start with a small cone or square. As you get more experienced, you can work with larger cones. Cut flowers or herbs with a short stem. You can use indoor or outdoor flowers, fresh or dried. If you use fresh flowers, you will have to replace them because flowers fade. Only use those with firm stems; otherwise you will need to tie the stems to a toothpick to poke them into the Styrofoam.

Stick the flowers and herb stems into the cone. If you want to add some ribbons, tie bows around bobby pins. That way they poke in easier. Leave the Styrofoam cone bottom empty so it will stand upright.

What you need

1 a Styrofoam cone

2 herbs

3 flowers with short stems

4 ribbon

5 bobby pins

How to use

The cones look wonderful at Christmas, and make great gifts. Add a Christmas star, Santa, or angel on top. There are many other Styrofoam shapes you can find at hobby stores. They can be used for Easter, perhaps with a bunny or other plastic decoration on top, and for other holidays.

Holiday tree

What to do

Make a totem pole base out of the modeling clay. Press the bottom of your totem pole stick in this base. Let it dry. The pole should stand firmly upright.

Have an adult help you split very rounded nuts, such as walnuts, in half. Take the nut from the shell. You will use the shell on your totem pole. First, glue seeds in place on each nutshell to make eyes and a nose. Paint a scary or animal face on each shell. You can make pointy teeth with white seeds. When the paint dries, glue the shells to the stick.

The smallest nut should be on top, the biggest on the bottom. If you use a whole nut that is too round to stick well, add some clay to the back to make it flat. Glue the nut to the clay first and let it dry.

What you need

1 shell nuts of different types and sizes

2 small seeds

3 modeling clay

4 white glue

5 finger paint and a brush

6 a 1-inch (2.5-centimeter) wide piece of wood, at least 6 inches (15 centimeters) long

Totem pole

What to do

Glue the pinecone bottom into the jar. It should fit snugly, as this holds the tree upright. Now paint the pinecone lightly with white glue. Right away, sprinkle gold, silver, or other holiday glitter over the cone. Let it dry at least an hour.

In the meantime, make tiny balls from the aluminum foil. These are your Christmas tree balls. Glue them onto the tree. If you can find a few small gummed stars, like those teachers use on home-work, you can glue these to your tree top.

You want to hide the tree bottom holder. You can wrap aluminum foil around it, or glue on some pretty Christmas wrapping paper.

What you need

1 large pinecones

2 white glue

3 shiny holiday glitter

4 aluminum foil

5 an empty short round jar or small box

6 a skinny paintbrush

7 shiny stick-on stars

Christmas tree

What to do

It's easy to make a square wreath. Wrap heavy-duty thread around small groups of cuttings. Then have an adult help you form a wire coat hanger into a square. Using the thread, fasten the wrapped herb bunches around the coat hanger. The top of the hanger makes a hanging hook. Tie pretty bows around it.

If you want to make a dangling herb decoration, use a heavy cord. Attach the wrapped herb groups along the cord. Wherever there is a space, add a colorful bow. Then put on a piece of ribbon as a hanger.

To make a round wreath, it's easiest to buy a wire wreath frame from a craft shop or florist. Attach your herb groupings to the frame.

The color scheme is up to you. Gray or silvery herbs look very pretty as a base for more colorful flowers and berries. You can add bows or other items found inexpensively at craft or sewing stores.

What you need

1 thick green thread

2 4-inch (10-centimeter) long herb cuttings

3 ribbon

4 a wire coat hanger

5 cord

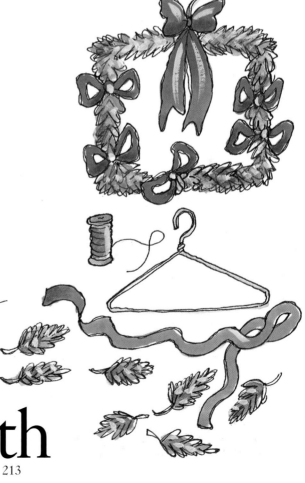

Herb wreath

213

Seed Catalogs: United States and Canada

United States:

Burpee Gardens
300 Park Avenue
Warminster, PA 18974

Ed Hume Seeds
PO Box 1450
Kent, WA 98035

Johnny's Selected Seeds
Foss Hill Road
Albion, ME 04910-9731

Mellingers
2310 W. South Range Road
North Lima, OH 44452-9731

Native Seeds/Search
2509 N. Campbell Avenue #325
Tucson, AZ 85719

Nichols Garden Nursery
1190 North Pacific Highway
Albany, OR 97321-4598

Park Seed
Cokesbury Road
Greenwood, SC 29647-0001

Pinetree Garden Seeds
Box 300
New Gloucester, ME 04260

Plants of the Southwest
Agua Fria, Rt 6 Box 11A
Santa Fe, NM 87505

Seeds of Change
1364 Rufina Circle #5
Santa Fe, NM 87501

Shepherd's Garden Seeds
6116 Highway 9
Felton, CA 95018

Southern Seeds
PO Box 2091
Melbourne, FL 32902

Stark Bro's Nurseries
Box 10
Louisiana, MO 63353-0010

Stokes Seeds
Box 548
Buffalo, NY 14240

Territorial Seed Company
20 Palmer Avenue
Cottage Grove, OR 97424

The Cook's Garden
PO Box 535
Londonderry, VT 05148-0535

Thompson & Morgan
PO Box 1308
Jackson, NJ 08527-0308

Vermont Bean Seed Company
Garden Lane
Fair Haven, VT 05743-0250

Temperatures across the United States vary greatly by state and within each state. Each of the above catalogs gives good descriptions. Planting times per area are noted on the seed packets, and may vary per seed type.

Because of changing mail and production costs, always inquire about catalog fees beforehand. The majority of catalogs cost under $3.

Canada:

Alberta Nurseries &
Seed Company
PO Box 20
Bowden, Alberta
Canada T0M 0K0

Butchart Gardens
Box 4010 Station A
Victoria, BC
Canada V8X 3X4

Dacha Barinka
25232 Strathcona Road
Chilliwack, BC
Canada V2P 3T2

Dominion Seed House
115 Guelph Street
Georgetown, Ontario
Canada L7G 4A2

Early's Farm & Garden Centre
PO Box 3024
2615 Lorne Avenue South
Saskatoon, Saskatchewan
Canada S7K 3S9

Gardenimport
PO Box 760
Thornhill, Ontario
Canada L3T 4A5

Island Seed Mail Order
PO Box 4278 Station A
Victoria, BC
Canada V8X 3XB

Rawlinson Garden Seed
269 College Road
Truro, Nova Scotia
Canada B2N 2P6

Richters
PO Box 26
Goodwood, Ontario
Canada L0C 1A0

Sanctuary Seeds
2388 West 4th Avenue
Vancouver, BC
Canada V6K 1P1

Seed Centre Ltd.
Box 3867 Station D
14510 127th Street
Edmonton, Alberta
Canada T5L 4K1

Stokes Seed Company
39 James Street
St. Catharines, Ontario
Canada L2R 6R6

Vesey's Seeds
PO Box 9000
Charlottetown, PE
Canada C0A 1P0

William Dam Seeds
PO Box 8400
278 Highway 8
Dundas, Ontario
Canada L9H 6M1

Canada is primarily a cool to moderate climate. The outdoor growing season is shorter than in many parts of the United States. Temperatures may drop to 0°F (-18°C) or below in winter.

Many Canadian seed companies will mail catalogs to the United States. There is sometimes an additional charge. Because of changing mail and production costs, always inquire about fees beforehand.

Glossary

Antennae paired feelers on the head of insects and crustaceans

Anther the end of the stamen. It contains pollen in pollen sacs.

Archaeologist a scientist who investigates the history of populations by examining any remains from earlier times

Artificial not real or natural

Bouquet several or many flowers fastened together

Bulb a stem base around one or more buds capable of developing into new plants

Calcium a mineral extremely important in bone health

Caravan a group of vehicles or animals traveling in a file

Commercial relating to business

Conqueror a winner in war, someone who overcomes by force

Corrugated bent into folds, wrinkled

Cultivation preparing land for crop raising

Dimension the length, width, or thickness of an item

Doily a small ornamental napkin

Edible anything that can be eaten for food

Evaporate to change into vapor or moisture

Fixative a substance that helps make something permanent

Folic acid necessary for healthy red blood cells in the body. A severe lack may cause specific anemia.

Formula a recipe or set way of stating something

Fragrance a sweet smell

Ingredient a part of any mixture

Insect most have one pair of antennae, three pairs of legs, three separate body parts, and wings

Interval a pause in time

Kiva a large Pueblo Indian ceremonial chamber

Lukewarm somewhat warm, but not hot

Magnifying glass a special piece of glass designed to make things look larger

Marsh an area of low and very wet land

Mildew many extremely tiny fungi growing on plants that produce a whitish discoloration

Mold extremely tiny fungi growing on animal or vegetable matter, giving it a furry appearance

Molt to shed, such as feathers or skin

Monastery a residence for persons who have taken religious vows

Mummy a human body dried up and preserved

Myth an invented story

Niacin (see vitamin B_3)

Ovule the portion of a seed plant that becomes a seed following fertilization of the egg-cell within

Pellagra a disease, caused by lack of dietary niacin, affecting the skin, digestive system, and nervous system

Phosphorus a mineral that is a necessary part of bone

Pistil the female part of a flower that will produce seeds

Plague a widespread disease with a high death rate

Pollen yellow, powdery grains produced in the male part of flowering plants

Potassium a mineral required for efficient body cell membrane functioning. Severe lack may cause muscle cramps.

Potpourri dried flower petals and spices kept in a container to provide fragrance

Pouch a bag or sack for small items

Prehistoric the time before written history began

Project a plan, or definite research study

Pyramid a construction with a square base and pointed top. Often used as a tomb, particularly in early Egypt.

Rafter a roof-support timber

Rhizome a rootlike stem

Riboflavin (see vitamin B_2)

Seedling a very young or small plant

Sentimental an emotional feeling, such as tenderness

Silica a hard, white, colorless material found in nature. Silica gel is a chemical compound that feels and looks like salt.

Silt a deposit of fine earth or mud left behind by moving waters

Spice a strongly flavored or fragrant substance of vegetable origin

Sprout to begin growing, as a plant from a seed

Stamen the pollen-carrying male part of a plant

Styrofoam the brand name for a lightweight chemically produced material

Superstition an unreasoning fear of the mysterious or unknown

Technique a way of doing a task

Totem an object or thing in nature that represents a related group of people, such as a tribe

Transplant to move from one place to another

Tribute a token, often money, given in gratitude or as payment from one government to another

Vaccination an injection usually given to prevent disease

Vitamin A necessary to normal body functioning. Severe lack may cause night blindness, lung problems, and other difficulties.

Vitamin B_1 (thiamin) the primary body use is as part of carbohydrate (sugar) metabolism. Severe lack may cause heart, nervous system, and muscle problems.

Vitamin B_2 (riboflavin) the primary body use is energy production

Vitamin B_3 (niacin) the primary body use is energy production. Severe lack may cause pellagra or mental symptoms.

Vitamin B_6 (pyridoxine) involved in red blood cell production, and manufacture of body proteins. Severe lack may cause nervous system problems.

Vitamin C necessary in the body process that produces collagen, a basic part of body supporting tissues. Also helps the body make necessary hormones for life processes. Severe lack causes scurvy.

Whorl shaped like a coil

Zodiac signs 12 astronomical constellations, believed by some to each have its own sign

Supplemental Reading

Baily, L. H. *How Plants Get Their Names*. New York: Dover Press, 1963.

Blose, Nora. *Herb-Drying Handbook*. New York: Sterling Publishers, 1993.

Bubel, Nancy. *The Adventurous Gardener*. Boston: David Godine, 1979.

Coon, Nelson. *Dictionary of Useful Plants*. Emmaus, Pennsylvania: Rodale, 1974.

Foster, Steven. *Herbal Bounty*. Salt Lake City: Peregrine Smith Books, 1984.

Fussell, Betty H. *The Story of Corn*. New York: Knopf, 1992.

Gordon, Lesley. *Green Magic*. New York: Viking Press, 1977.

Hall, Dorothy. *The Book of Herbs*. New York: Scribner's, 1972.

Haring, Elda. *The Complete Book of Growing Plants from Seed*. New York: Hawthorn Books, 1967.

Haughton, Claire. *Green Immigrants*. New York: Harcourt, Brace, Jovanovich, 1978.

Hobhouse, Henry. *Seeds of Change*. New York: Harper & Row, 1986.

Holt, Rackham. *George Washington Carver*. New York: Doubleday, 1963.

James, Wilma. *Gardening with Biblical Plants*. Chicago: Nelson-Hall, 1984.

Kalman, Bobbie. *Early Pleasures and Pastimes*. New York: Crabtree Pub, 1983

Krupp, Marcus. *Current Medical Diagnosis and Treatment*. Norwalk, Connecticut/San Mateo, California: Appleton & Lange, 1990.

Lore and Legend of Herbs and Spices. St. Louis, Missouri: St. Louis Herb Society, 1987.

McMair, James. *The World of Herbs & Spices*. San Francisco: Ortho Books, 1978.

Neithammer, Carolyn. *American Indian Food and Lore*. New York: MacMillan, 1974.

Nutritive Value of Foods. U.S. Government Printing Office, 1981.

Oster, Maggie. *The Potato Garden*. New York: Harmony Books, 1993.

Perper, Hazel. *Citrus Seed Grower's Indoor How-To*. New York: Dodd, Mead, 1971.

Plummer, Beverly. *Fragrance*. New York: Atheneum, 1975.

Powell, Horace B. *The Original Has This Signature—W. K. Kellogg*. Englewood Cliffs, New Jersey: Prentice Hall, 1956

Punch, Walter T. *Keeping Eden*. Boston: Bulfinch Press, 1992.

Raymond, Dick. *The Joy of Gardening*. Vermont: Garden Way, 1982.

Rohde, Eleanor. *Rose Recipes from Olden Times*. New York: Dover Books, 1973.

Root, Waverly. *Food, An Authoritative History*. New York: Simon & Schuster, 1980.

Rupp, Rebecca. *Blue Corn and Square Tomatoes*. Vermont: Garden Way, 1987.

Sharpe, J. E. *American Indian Cooking*. Cherokee, North Carolina: Cherokee Publishers, 1973.

Silverman, Harold. *The Vitamin Book*. New York: Bantam, 1985.

Sturtevant, Edward. *Edible Plants of the World*. New York: Dover Press, 1972.

Tannahill, Reay. *Food in History*. New York: Crown Publishers, 1989.

Thompson, Dorothea. *Creative Decorations with Dried Flowers*. New York: Hearthside Press, 1972.

Van Patten, George. *Organic Gardening Vegetables*. Portland, Oregon: Van Patten Publishing, 1991.

Walker, Winifred. *All the Plants of the Bible*. London: Lutterworth Press, 1958.

Weschler, Herman. *Gods and Goddesses in Art and Legend*. New York: Washington Square Press, 1960.

Williamson, Darcy. *Cooking With Spirit*. Bend, Oregon: Maverick Publishers, 1987.

Index